COLLINS GEM
ANTIQUE
MARKS

*a mine of information*

D1578598

COLLINS GEM
D

COLLINS GEM
CRICKET

*a mine of information*

COLLINS GEM
DIETING

*a mine of information*

COLLINS GEM
DOGS

*a mine of information*

COLLINS GEM
FIRST AID

*a mine of information*

COLLINS GEM
INTERNET

Connect

COLLINS GEM
PREDICTING

*a mine of information*

COLLINS GEM
Ready
REFERENCE

*a mine of information*

COLLINS GEM
SHARKS

COLLINS GEM
WHALES
& DOLPHINS

*a mine of information*

COLLINS GEM
WHISKY

*a mine of information*

COLLINS GEM
WORD
PROCESSING

*a mine of information*

COLLINS GEM
Your PC

*a mine of information*

# COLLINS GEM

# COMPUTER JARGON

**David Townsend Jones**

HarperCollins*Publishers*

David Townsend Jones has been using computers since the mid-1980s, when they first reached the desks of professional editors. His Cardiff-based company, Adastra Publishing Limited, specializes in providing content for Internet and multimedia projects.
He can be contacted at: davidtj@adastrawales.demon.co.uk

HarperCollins*Publishers*
Westerhill Road, Bishopbriggs, Glasgow G64 2QT

First published 2000

Reprint 10 9 8 7 6 5 4 3 2 1 0

© Book Creation Services Ltd, 2000
This book was created by Book Creation Services Ltd
for HarperCollins*Publishers* Ltd

ISBN 0 00 472484-4

Printed in Italy by Amadeus S.p.A.

# Preface

Every day, new people start computing. The young, with their natural tendency to plunge straight in and get on with it, have little fear of jargon. But the world of mature adults – even senior adults – is fast tuning in to computing too. Few of us want to feel excluded from the revolution that information technology is bringing, unavoidably, to all our lives.

But for older novices, jargon may be a real barrier. How do they decipher those jargon-crammed ads? What are those young sales people actually talking about? What does 'digital' mean, for heaven's sake? Why do you 'boot' a computer? What is 'debugging'? Some poor folk may be too embarrassed to admit they still think a window is for looking through, or that a mouse mat is for a small rodent with clean habits. And then there's all those acronyms: DVD, MP3, BIOS, PIM, SDRAM… .

Don't panic! This little book is what you beginners from the real world need as you dip your first toes into the great, thrilling world of computing. Here you will find simple, stripped-down explanations, written in plain, layman's English, extensively cross-referenced (in bold) and illustrated, of the 750 or so most common, essential computing terms. Keep *Collins Gem Computer Jargon* by your side, and soon you too will be holding your own, and finding that none of this is as difficult as you first feared.

# A

**A:** What your **floppy disk drive** (FDD) is called by your PC under MS-DOS and Windows. If you have two FDDs of different sizes, the second is usually called B:

**abort**   **1.** To stop a program or computer command yourself, before it has finished naturally.   **2.** The term also covers an unexpected termination by the computer because of a **bug** or malfunction.

**About dialogue box** Information about a program's name, version number and other details, found in the Windows **Help** menu.

**accessory**   **1.** Bits and pieces used with your computer, such as **mouse** mats and screen filters. **2.** Windows uses the name 'Accessories' for its in-built set of **utilities** and **applets**. Mac OS calls them 'desk accessories'.

**access time**   The measure of the speed of a **hard disk drive**. A low access time indicates a fast hard drive. When making comparisons, look for 'memory access time' (measured in nanoseconds) and/or 'disk access time' (measured in milliseconds). Sometimes the speed of a disk drive is measured by the rate at which it transfers data – in this case, a higher 'data transfer rate' indicates a faster drive.

**account**   If you are connected to a **network** then you have an account. This logs the details of your computer and governs the conditions under which you may access resources, such as shared data or printers, on the network.

**accounting software**   Programs that perform accounting functions, such as tracking income and expenditure, running a payroll, invoicing, etc. Sophisticated business packages include *Sage* and *QuickBooks*, while simpler personal accounting packages include *Quicken* and *Microsoft Money*.

**active**   Refers to the current focus of attention, such as the active **window** in which you are currently working, the active **cell** in a **spreadsheet**, or the active **file** that you have on the screen before you.

**Active Desktop**   A feature of Windows 98 and **Internet Explorer** 4 (and upwards) that allows you to

*Microsoft's Active Desktop, showing the Channel Bar*

set up the Windows **desktop** to display information downloaded from the Internet. It can also be configured to **download** updated information automatically.

**adaptor**   A piece of hardware that plugs into a computer, usually through an **expansion slot**, to add new features or improve performance, such as connection to a **network**, better video **resolution**, or access to a **scanner**. Also called **expansion board** and **expansion card**.

**add-in, add-on**   **1.** A software program that extends the capabilities of a larger program.   **2.** A hardware component that enhances the capabilities of a computer or other device, for example to add **memory** to a PC or printer.

**address**   **1.** Shorthand for an **e-mail address**. **2.** On the Internet, shorthand for an **IP Address**, which locates the computer hosting a **Website**. Also known as an **URL**.   **3.** A name or label identifying a computer or other device on a **network**. **4.** The location on a computer or network of some particular information, expressed as a unique series of numbers.

*A typical PIM address book page*

**address book**    A place to store and retrieve **e-mail** addresses in an e-mail program, or other contact information in a **personal information manager** (PIM).

*The Eudora Light e-mail address book*

**administrator**    The human manager of a **network** or database.

**Adobe Systems**    A leading provider of graphic design, publishing and imaging software for Web and print production. Responsible for **PostScript**, the universal page description language; Adobe Type Manager, the PostScript font utility; the **desktop publishing** programs *InDesign*, *PageMaker* and *FrameMaker*; the graphics package *Illustrator*; the photo manipulation program *PhotoShop*; and *Acrobat*, for creating portable electronic documents (*see* **PDF**).

**alert box**   A **message box** that delivers a warning on-screen, for example if you try to quit a program before saving your data.

**alias**   On a Macintosh, an alias allows a document or program to be shared from different locations, using different names if desired. In Windows, the term **shortcut** is used.

**alignment**   The positioning of text relative to the left and right margins.

**Left-aligned text**

| |
|---|
| Right-aligned text |
| Centred text |
| Justified text stretches or contracts to fill the space between the margins. Justified text stretches or contracts to fill the space between the margins. |

*You can align text in various ways*

**Alt key**   A **modifier key** you press in combination with other keys to give commands to the computer.

**analogue**   Refers to information in a continuous form, meaning that it changes constantly, as in a clock with hands. Compare with **digital** information, as in a clock that shows time every tenth of a second. Almost all modern computers are digital.

**antivirus**   A utility designed to look out for and remove a computer **virus** program. Popular examples are Dr Solomon's Anti-Virus Toolkit, Norton Antivirus and McAfee VirusScan.

**Apple Computer**  Manufacturer of the influential **Macintosh** family of computers and the Mac OS operating system, which popularized the windows-and-icon-based **GUI** as the standard interface between computer and operator.

**Apple key**  A **modifier key**, labelled with the Apple logo, on a Macintosh keyboard. Synonymous with the **Command key**.

**Apple menu**  The menu reached via the tiny Apple icon at the top left of a **Macintosh** screen. This menu generally displays various **accessories** and small programs such as the calculator, although you can add other **aliases**, such as for your favourite programs.

**applet**  **1.** A small program for specific functions, which usually come with the **operating system**. Examples in Windows are Paint and Notepad. On a Macintosh, examples are Calculator and Scrapbook. **2.** In **Java**, an applet is a mini-program embedded in a Web document. When the document is downloaded, the Java applet runs the program automatically.

**AppleTalk**  An inexpensive but relatively slow system developed by **Apple Computer** to **network** both Macintosh and IBM PC computers. An AppleTalk port is built in to all Macs.

**application**  Used loosely as another word for 'program', although specifically it means a program with which you can do something useful with your computer, such as writing or keeping accounts. Compare with **utility** programs, which help you maintain your computer.

**archive**    **1.** A directory, disk or tape where important files you want to keep are stored for future access. **2.** A file, equivalent to a **folder**, containing one or more **compressed files**.

**arrow keys**    Keys that move the **cursor** on-screen, left, right, up and down. Larger movements are achieved by combining arrow keys with appropriate **modifier keys**. They form part of the **cursor keys**.

**ASCII**    Stands for American Standard Code for Information Interchange (pronounced 'as-key'). This is a standard set of characters understood by all computers, consisting mostly of letters and numbers plus a few basic symbols such as $ and %.

**associate**    When you command your computer to open a file, it needs to associate the file with the program in which it was created. In the Mac OS, this information is stored automatically when you create the file. In Windows, association is based on three-letter file **extensions**. For example, .doc files are associated with *Microsoft Word*, and .wpd files with *WordPerfect*.

**attached file**    A file attached to an **e-mail** message. Formatted files, such as *Microsoft Word* documents or **compressed files**, must be encoded before they are sent and decoded when received. Modern e-mail programs generally handle this automatically.

**AUTOEXEC.BAT**     A file that Windows-based PCs run automatically when started up. It gives the computer various basic instructions about starting Windows, running **antivirus** checks in the background, identifying the keyboard, and so on. *See also* **CONFIG.SYS**.

**autosave**     In most Windows programs, you can set your PC to autosave your files (save them automatically) at intervals specified by you – say, every five minutes. That way, if your computer crashes or loses power, you won't lose more than a few minutes' work.

# B

**Back button**   A **button** on **Web browser** software used to return to the previous **Web page** you visited. In Windows 98, **Windows Explorer** also features a back button.

**background**   **1.** Modern computers can **multitask**, allowing you to give a command and leave the computer to get on with the task while you switch to some other activity. For example, you can write a letter while an earlier letter is being printed in the background or an e-mail is being sent. **2.** Another term for **wallpaper**.

**backslash**   The \ key on your keyboard is called the 'backslash'. It is used as a separator in a **pathname** in MS-DOS and Windows.

**Backspace key**   Moves the cursor on-screen to the left, deleting text as it moves. Press it once to delete one character; keep pressing to delete continuously till you decide to stop.

**backup, backup program**   A copy of a file made for security reasons, in case of accidental loss or **corruption**. Also used as a verb: 'to backup'. 'Backup your data regularly' is a golden rule of computing. Various backup programs are available, using removable disks or tapes, which often compress the files automatically to make best use of storage space.

**bandwidth**    The amount of data a computer connection, such as a telephone connection to the Internet or a network connection, can handle in one second. As usual in computing, more means better. Measured in **bits per second** (**bps**) or **megahertz** (MHz).

**banner ad**    A box running across a **Web page**, containing an advertisement.

*A typical banner ad*

**baud, baud rate**    A baud is the number of signalling elements per second sent by a communications device such as a modem. In theory, a modem with a high baud rate means fast transmission. In practice, speed is determined by the weakest link: a noisy phone line, or a slower modem at the receiving end. *See also* **bits per second (bps)**.

**BIOS**    Acronym for Basic Input/Output System, a set of basic programs stored on a chip. The computer runs these each time it starts up, to make sure it is functioning properly and to instruct the **hard disk**, keyboard and monitor to handle data.

**bit**    Short for 'binary digit', the smallest unit of information handled by a computer. A binary digit can be one of a pair: 1 (on) or 0 (off), yes or no, etc. The ability to distinguish these accurately forms the basis of computer circuitry. The ability of a **microprocessor** to process data is measured by the number of bits it can process at one time.

**bitmap, bitmap graphic**   A bitmap is an image displayed on the screen dot by dot. Each dot is called a

*A bitmap graphic*

**pixel**. Bitmap graphics can be created or edited in a **paint program**. *Compare with* **vector graphic**.

**bits per second (bps)** A measurement of data transmission speed. Most important as a measure of the speed of a **modem**: a bps rating of 57.6K (K meaning 1,000) represents an average transmission speed of 57,600 bits per second.

**blind carbon copy (BCC)**   A copy of an e-mail message sent to someone without the knowledge of the main recipient. Contrast with **carbon copy**. Both terms date from the typewriter era.

**bold**   A form of **typeface** in which text prints darker and heavier, **like this**.

**bookmark**   **1.** In a **Web browser** such as **Netscape Navigator**, to record a **Website** or **Web page** you want to revisit later. In **Internet Explorer**, this is termed a **Favorite**. **2.** In a word processor document, a code you insert to which you can jump at a later point – a passage for rewriting, for example.

**Boolean** Boolean logic, a branch of mathematics, deals with two alternative values (true or false) and is used to design computer circuits, which are likewise based on distinguishing two alternative values (1 or 0, etc.). A Boolean search, for example a query to a database, uses operators (expressions) like OR, AND or NOT to focus the search.

| If you link two search terms with: | The search result is: |
| --- | --- |
| AND ('Arsenal AND Chelsea') | Only items that contain both these terms |
| OR ('Arsenal OR Chelsea') | Any item that contains either of these terms |
| NOT ('Arsenal NOT Chelsea') | Any item that contains 'Arsenal', except those that also contain 'Chelsea' |

*Boolean operators*

**boot** To start a computer. A cold boot involves starting from the off position. A warm boot, faster and gentler, involves resetting a computer that is already switched on. Short for 'bootstrap', implying the quaint notion that the computer has to 'pull itself up by the bootstraps'.

**boot disk**   The disk from which you boot or start
your computer. This is normally the hard disk, but if
that fails, a floppy disk with the essential elements of the
operating system can be used to start the machine. In
Windows 95/98, making a boot disk (called a **startup
disk**) is straightforward.

**bps**   Acronym for **bits per second**.

**Briefcase**   A Windows 95/98 feature that allows you
to transfer files between two PCs (for example, a
desktop machine and a portable machine) and to
synchronize them so that both machines hold the most
recent versions.

*A Browse dialogue box*

**browse, browsing**   **1.** To look for something on your hard disk, often via a **button** or **dialogue box** that allows you to move up or down one level at a time. **2.** To use a **Web browser**.

**bubble-jet printer**   Developed by Canon as a variation on the **inkjet printer**, a bubble-jet heats the ink to form a bubble, which shoots the ink from tiny nozzles onto the paper.

**buffer**   A portion of **memory** used for temporary storage. For example, when you press several keys in quick succession on the keyboard, the commands are stored momentarily in a buffer, allowing the computer to process them in the correct order. Laser printers have large buffers, which hold information until the printer is ready to print, so that the computer is not tied up with print jobs.

**bug**   An error in a program that prevents it from working properly. The complexity of computer programming, combined with commercial pressures to meet production deadlines, results in nearly all programs having some bugs.

**bullet**   A small graphic used to set off each item in a list, such as a solid dot (•), a hollow diamond (◊), a heart (♥), or whatever you choose.

**bulletin board**   A bulletin board system (BBS) is an electronic message centre on the Web, where you can leave a message to which others can respond. Often accessed by password, bulletin boards usually serve particular interest groups such as fan clubs or users of a software program.

**bundled software**    Software that supposedly comes free when you buy a computer or other hardware. Included (bundled) will be software you need (like the operating system) or may not need (games, etc.).

**bus**    Comes in different flavours: data bus, address bus, control bus and **expansion bus**. Collectively they form an electrical pathway, essentially a collection of wires, along which signals travel from one part of the computer to another. With buses, more width is good – a 32-bit bus transmits more data than a 16-bit one. More speed (measured in **megahertz**) is also good.

**button**    You **click** on a button in a **dialogue box** to execute a command, choose an option, open a further dialogue box or just cancel the whole thing, using the mouse.

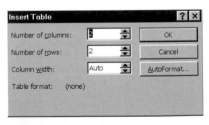

*A three-button dialogue box*

**byte**   Computers need combinations of **bits**, each
of which represents 1 (on) or 0 (off), to define
complex information. The byte, equal to eight bits,
is regarded as the basic unit of measurement for
computer storage. Each byte stores the equivalent
of one character (a letter, number or symbol). *See
also* **kilobyte**, **megabyte** *and* **gigabyte**.

# C

**C:** What your **hard disk drive** (HDD) is called by your PC under MS-DOS and Windows. If you have two hard drives, the second is usually called D:, and so on down to Z:

**cache**   Acting rather like a **buffer**, a cache is a high-speed store-and-retrieve area in which information you access repeatedly is held by the computer, to save processing time.

**CAD**   Acronym for computer-aided design. CAD programs are used by professionals such as designers, architects and engineers for precise calculation and three-dimensional visualization of products and their components. The best-known package is *AutoCAD*.

|   | A | B | C |
|---|---|---|---|
| 1 | Analysis of Mrs Jones's pets | | |
| 2 | Type of pet | Number | |
| 3 | Cats | 14 | |
| 4 | Dogs | 8 | |
| 5 | Budgies | 33 | |
| 6 | Parrots | 2 | |
| 7 | Hamsters | 88 | |
| 8 | Goldfish | 13 | |
| 9 | TOTAL | 158 | |

*A spreadsheet calculation*

**calculate**   To perform a mathematical operation, such as in a **spreadsheet**.

**Calculator**   Both Windows and Mac OS come with an **accessory** called Calculator, which is exactly like a simple pocket calculator.

**Cancel button**   Most **dialogue boxes**, both in Windows and Mac OS, have a Cancel button, which allows you to close the box without applying any choices. Usually, pressing the **Esc key** has the same effect.

**Caps Lock key**   Press it to type repeated capital – or **uppercase** – letters without having to use the **Shift key**. You still need to press Shift for the symbols on top of other keys. Usually a light comes on somewhere on the keyboard when Caps Lock is 'on'.

**carbon copy (CC)**   A copy of an e-mail message sent to someone in addition to the main recipient. This is recorded on the message header and is therefore made known to all. Sometimes called a 'courtesy copy'. *Contrast with* **blind carbon copy**.

**case-sensitive**   Meaning that it is essential to type a command or address in **lowercase** or **uppercase**, or an exact combination of the two. Generally, typed computer commands are not case-sensitive. However, network and Internet **passwords** *are* case-sensitive.

**CD Player**   Windows PCs can play audio CDs using an **accessory** called CD Player. The control buttons are similar to those on a stereo system. The Mac OS equivalent is AppleCD Audio Player.

*The Windows CD Player*

**CD-ROM, CD-R, CD-RW**    CD-ROM is the acronym for Compact Disk Read-Only Memory, a **read-only** storage medium that holds huge quantities of data such as an entire encyclopaedia, or complex multi-module programs such as Microsoft **Office**. A CD-R is a recordable CD that can only be recorded upon once. A CD-RW is also recordable but allows an unlimited number of recordings.

**cell, cell address**    In a **table** or **spreadsheet**, a cell is the rectangle at the intersection of a vertical column and horizontal row. A spreadsheet cell address is identified by the column letter and row number: thus cell E3 is in the third row of the fifth column. Another term is 'coordinate'.

**central processing unit (CPU)**    The brain of the computer; the **microprocessor** chip that controls everything. Often referred to as the 'central processor', or just 'processor'. The capabilities of the whole computer are determined by the power of the CPU.

**centre**    To align text in the middle of the page, so that the centre-point of each line is equidistant from the left and right margins or boundaries. The American spelling 'center' is used in most software.

**channel**    When you **log on** to the Internet, channels to which you subscribe can automatically deliver content from selected Websites directly to your computer. Different channels deliver different kinds of information, such as sport, news or travel conditions. However, not all Web browsers support the Microsoft channel system.

**Channel Bar**   By default, **Internet Explorer** 4.0 and
5.0 install a Channel Bar on the left side of the
Windows 95/98 **desktop**. This provides easy access to
the **channels** available in different categories. It is
possible to remove this bar.

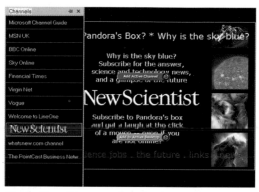

*Use the Channel Bar to view channels and subscribe to them*

**character**   Any letter, number, symbol or
punctuation you can type from your keyboard is
a character.

**chat, chat room**   On the Net, you chat to another
person by typing at them, whereupon s/he types back at
you, and so on. Several people can participate in a chat

session. Although a crude form of conversation, online chatting is enormously popular. A chat room is a named site dedicated to a specific interest group or topic.

**check box**    In a **dialogue box**, a small box you click to select or deselect an option. Checked (marked) means 'Yes please'; unchecked (empty) means 'No thank you'.

**chip**    A tiny electronic circuit on a silicon wafer. Numerous chips, the **CPU** chief among them, run your computer. Today's Pentium and PowerPC chips are the low-cost equivalent of a multi-million-pound mainframe computer of the 1970s.

**Chooser**    A Mac desk **accessory**, found in the **Apple menu**, which allows you to choose your printer and turn **AppleTalk** on or off.

**click**    **1.** What you do with a **mouse button**. *See also* **double-click**.    **2.** To select an item or carry out an action by placing the mouse **pointer** in a **button** or **menu** choice on-screen and clicking the mouse button – as in: 'Please click on File, then Open.'

**client**    **1.** In a **network**, a client computer can request something, such as a data file or access to a printer, from a **server** computer.    **2.** A program that communicates with a server located on the Internet, for example to obtain a Web document or exchange e-mail messages.

**clip art**    Ready-made artwork that you can insert into documents. The term derives from traditional books of graphics, which layout artists clipped out to decorate

*The Clip Gallery in Word 97*

their layouts. Modern word processors and desktop publishing programs come with ample clip art, and much more is available from the Net.

**Clipboard** When you copy or cut something to be pasted in somewhere else, the computer holds it in memory on the Clipboard. Only one item at a time can be stored on the Clipboard. In Windows 98, the current item can be seen in View Clipboard; some Mac programs have a similar facility.

**clock rate, clock speed** Interchangeable terms for the speed of the **CPU**, measured in **megahertz** (MHz).

Generally speaking, the higher the clock speed, the faster the computer.

**clone**    Once used of any **IBM-compatible** computer not actually manufactured by IBM. Now largely meaningless in the sprawling **PC** world. Apple Computer, however, only allowed its operating system to be run on Mac-compatible machines comparatively recently, so the term 'Mac clone' still retains significance.

**close, close box, close button**    You close a **window** to remove it from the screen, usually using the graphical close box (or close button). This may also involve closing the whole program. There are other ways to close a program, including the Close or Exit command in the File **menu** (or whichever menu is found on the extreme left of the **menu bar**).

**code**    To write a computer program or set of instructions for a computer. The written program itself is also referred to as 'code'.

**collapse**    In a Windows Explorer **folder tree**, the opposite of **expand**: what you do when you hide the contents of a folder or subfolder.

**command**    An instruction to a computer, executed by choosing an option from a menu, pressing a function key, typing a command, or another action. Examples are Print, Save, Paste, Undo, Check Spelling and Exit.

**command-driven, command line**    Command-driven software is controlled by typing successive instructions on a command line (such as the **DOS**

```
C:\WINDOWS>copy a:*.mdb d:\temp
Overwrite d:\temp\CompJarg.mdb (Yes/No/All)?y
        1 file(s) copied

C:\WINDOWS>d:

D:\Windows 95 Data>cd ..\temp

D:\Temp>dir *.mdb

 Volume in drive D has no label
 Volume Serial Number is 307C-37A2
 Directory of D:\Temp

COMPJARG MDB        804,864  20/10/99   1:29 CompJarg.mdb
        1 file(s)         804,864 bytes
        0 dir(s)    1,962,475,520 bytes free

D:\Temp>del *.mdb
```

*MS-DOS commands*

prompt). It is fast and flexible, but you get no help from
the computer. Contrast with **menu-driven** software,
which is easier to use but more cumbersome.

**Command key**    A modifier key, labelled with a
cloverleaf symbol, on a Macintosh keyboard. On all but
the oldest Apples it is synonymous with the **Apple key**.

**compatible, compatibility**    The ability of one
computing thing to work with another. In principle, **PC**
devices like printers are compatible with all PCs. With
some technical expertise, PCs and Macs can be made
mostly compatible; without it, they remain largely
strangers. 'Backward-compatible' software will run
older versions of the software. 'Upward-compatible'
hardware claims to be designed with the future in mind
(though only time will tell).

**compressed files, compression**    Compressing a
file means reducing the amount of disk storage space or

transmission time it needs. Special **utilities** such as WinZip for Windows and StuffIt for the Mac compress or **zip** files and **unzip** them in reverse.

**compute** To use a computer; to calculate an answer; or (colloquially) to make sense, as in: 'That computes,' or, more usually: 'That doesn't compute.'

**computer** A device that can be programmed to accept and process data, perform complex calculations and much else, based on instructions given to it by you, its human operator. (Always remember: you're the boss.)

**computer graphics** Anything visual on a computer: **clip art**, business graphs and charts, photographs, something created in a **paint program**, etc.

**conferencing** Several people sharing a document over the Internet – for example, when drafting a business proposal. Each person can amend the document directly, using a **chat** screen to exchange comments and ideas. *See also* **video conferencing**.

**CONFIG.SYS** A file that Windows-based PCs run automatically when started up. It gives the computer various basic instructions about starting Windows and working with equipment like the CD-ROM drive. *See also* **AUTOEXEC.BAT**.

**configure** To set up a piece of hardware or software so that it works in the way you or your computer want. Even in these days of **Plug and Play** automation, you are still asked to make choices.

**context-sensitive help**    Help that addresses whatever you are doing at the moment. In most Windows programs, pressing Shift + F1 will add a question mark to the mouse cursor; point this at an on-screen item to get information about it. Or, Shift+F1

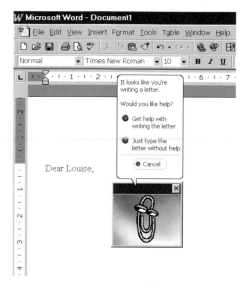

*Context-sensitive help: the (in)famous Office paperclip*

arouses a graphical help feature, in which you type a question and it endeavours to offer a range of relevant help topics.

**Control Panel**    A window full of icons, which allow you to modify different aspects of a computer's operation, found in the Windows, Mac and OS/2 operating systems.

**conventional memory**    The first 640K of **RAM**, which under **MS-DOS** was the only portion of memory that programs could use (the rest being reserved for MS-DOS itself). Until a few years ago, this restriction limited the performance capability of most PCs, but newer operating systems have made the issue irrelevant.

**cookie**    A simple text file saved to your **hard disk** by a **Web page**. It stores information about you such as your identity, or perhaps a record of the areas of the Web page that interested you. When you revisit, the page will read the cookie and may attempt to present you with tailor-made information.

**coordinate**    Another term for **cell address**.

**copy, copy and paste**    **1.** The command that copies something, such as a paragraph, graphic or row of numbers, to **paste** into a different location. The copy is stored on the **Clipboard**.    **2.** Creating a duplicate of a file. You can then rename the file and recycle all its contents.

**corruption**    Damage to data. Corruption spells trouble. Time to get your **backup** out (assuming you have followed the golden rule).

**CPU** Acronym for **central processing unit**.

**crash** An unexpected program **abort** or, more seriously, the ceasing to function of the whole computer (also known as a **system freeze**). When the former happens, launch the program again. When it's the latter, **restart** the computer. If either still won't work, seek help.

**Ctrl-Alt-Delete** The key combination that **reboots** the computer, for example after a **crash**. For the Mac equivalents, *see* **system freeze**.

**Ctrl key** A **modifier key** you press in combination with other keys to give commands to the computer.

**cursor** **1.** A symbol blinking on the screen to show where the next **character** will be typed. It can be moved with the mouse or with the **arrow keys**. **2.** Another term for the mouse **pointer**.

**cursor keys** Keys that let you move the **cursor** around: on a PC keyboard these are the **arrow keys**, **Home key** and **End key**, and **Page Up/Page Down keys**. On older PC keyboards, the **numeric keypad** doubled up, sometimes confusingly, as the cursor keys.

On modern PC and Mac keyboards there are separate banks of cursor keys.

**customize**    To choose, from the various options offered by a program, which features you want, or how you want it to look and behave. Modern software is highly customizable.

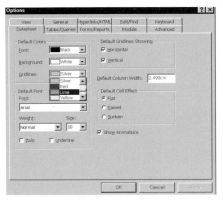

*Options in Microsoft Access, here customizing the appearance of the database*

**cut, cut and paste**    **1.** The command that cuts (removes) something, such as a sentence, table or illustration, from its current location. You can then paste it into a different location, or into another

document. Once cut, it is stored on the **Clipboard**.
**2.** Moving a file from its current location to a new one.

**cyberspace** Nowhere and everywhere, cyberspace is where computers and their users interact and trade information without physically meeting. It is a nickname for the vast online world of the Internet.

# D

**DAT** Acronym for Digital Audio Tape, a high-capacity magnetic tape used mainly for **backups**. Refers also to the type of drive that reads and records the tape.

**data** Data is information you put into your computer. You then use the computer to process the data: edit, design, calculate, analyse, sort into alphabetical order, etc. Finally you command the computer where and how to store your data.

**database** A collection of information (**data**), separated into its components. Stored in a special program, it allows you quickly to sort or select specific components. A simple example is a national database of addresses, comprising people's names, street addresses, towns and postal codes. In a database, you might sort these by town, or extract a list of all the Smiths, or pinpoint all the Smiths who live in Halifax. Popular programs include *Microsoft Access* and *FileMaker*.

**data compression** Storing data in a form that requires less space. Compressed files save online time because they can be transmitted more quickly. They also take up less space on a hard disk or in an **archive**. They must be decompressed before you can use them again.

**debug, debugger**
The debugger's mission
is to find **bugs** (errors)
in a computer program
and remove them.

**decrypt, decryption**
Decoding – the
opposite of **encryption**,
which is coding data
into a secret format, for

security. Decryption turns it back into its original
and useful form.

**default**    What the computer assumes unless you
tell it otherwise. For example, Windows makes My
Documents the default folder for all your data. In
Britain, printers are set to a default paper size of 'A4
210 x 297 mm' and are confused by many pages created
in the US, where the default is 'Letter 8½ x 11 in'.

**defragment**    To make good the process of
**fragmentation**, the natural tendency of some **operating
systems** to scatter pieces of files all around a disk.
Unless this is periodically fixed, the computer will
gradually slow down.

**delete, Delete key**    To remove or erase a file or a
piece of data, by choosing the Delete option on-screen
or pressing the Delete key.

**desktop**    In a **GUI** interface, the desktop is what you
work on. Like a real desktop, you can decorate it to
your own taste. It holds **icons** representing programs or

## The Windows 95/98 desktop

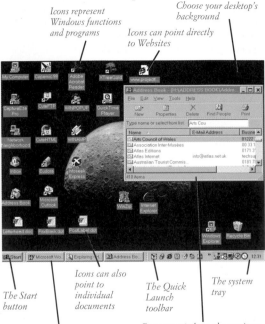

*Icons represent Windows functions and programs*

*Icons can point directly to Websites*

*Choose your desktop's background*

*The Start button*

*Icons can also point to individual documents*

*The Quick Launch toolbar*

*The system tray*

*Open programs sit on the Windows taskbar*

*Program windows always sit on the desktop (even if maximized to fill the whole screen)*

files, which you can move about or throw away, again like a real desktop. Program **windows** sit on top of it, and at its border sit key functions, such as the Windows **taskbar**.

**desktop computer**   One that sits on a desk, usually with the monitor on top of the computer box. Not a **tower** or **minitower** PC, or a **portable computer**.

*Computers come in various shapes and sizes*

**desktop publishing (DTP)**   Creating print- or Web-ready publications that integrate text and graphics. Full-blown DTP packages such as *QuarkXPress*, Adobe's *InDesign* and *FrameMaker*, and Corel's *Ventura* allow precise control of typefaces, placement of illustrations, indexing and other details. The best-known budget package is Microsoft's *Publisher*. Modern **word processors** also have DTP capabilities, but lack the precision and versatility of dedicated programs.

**destination**    The location to which you transfer data when you copy or move it. The location you take it from is the **source**.

**device, device driver**    A device is any hardware attached to the computer, whether internal (such as disk drives or the CD-ROM), integral to its operation (such as the monitor or keyboard) or external (such as a printer, mouse or modem). Interchangeable with the longer term 'peripheral device'. Most of them are controlled by a 'device driver', a special program loaded when the computer starts.

**diagnostic program**    Any **utility** that tells you what is in your computer or why it isn't working properly. Network **administrators** run them to check the performance of their network.

**dialogue box**    An on-screen 'box' that permits a dialogue between you and your software. It presents you with options, and you tell it your choices. (In software of American origin, the US spelling 'dialog' will be encountered.) In menus, options followed by an ellipsis (...) bring up a dialogue box. Menu options without ellipses **execute** (take effect) directly.

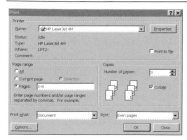

*Word's Printer dialogue box*

**Dial-Up Networking**   A Windows feature that connects your computer to another computer, via the phone and a **modem**. It can also be used to connect to the Internet via your **ISP**. The information is stored so that next time the connection is automatic.

**digital**   Refers to information transmitted in discontinuous form, as in a clock that shows the time every tenth of a second. Compare with **analogue** information, which is continuous. Almost all modern computers are digital, in that essentially they distinguish between just two values, 0 and 1, or off and on (*see* **bit**). They are able to convert analogue (continuous) information into digital (discontinuous) form and back again, as in digital audio on CDs.

**digital camera**   A camera that saves its photographs in **digital** form. They can then be transferred directly to your computer, where you can process and print them, add them to documents, put them on your Web page, and so on.

*Dingbats*

**DIMM**   Acronym for Dual Inline Memory Module, a kind of memory chip (or **RAM**).

**dimmed**   The same thing as **greyed out**: you cannot choose a command or option when it is dimmed.

**dingbats**   A font consisting of graphical symbols.

**directory**   **1.** Another word for **folder**. The term 'directory' is still widely used in PCs, although the folder concept is much more readily understood.   **2.** On the Internet, a comprehensive hierarchical collection of pre-researched Websites, grouped by topic and presented with short descriptions. Generally, a quicker way to find a quality site on a particular topic than a do-it-yourself search.

**disk, diskette**   The most common computer data storage medium. Usually spelled with a 'k' in computer contexts, the term actually covers most **media** you can use with a computer: a **hard disk**, a **floppy disk** (sometimes called a diskette), a **CD-ROM** disk, a **Jaz disk** or **Zip disk**, etc. The term is also extended to cover solid-state memory cards used in **palmtop computers**.

**disk controller**   The hardware that operates a **disk drive** and manages the flow of information between it and the **CPU**.

**disk drive**   A machine that reads **disks** and writes
onto them. On PCs, the computer names them A–Z. On
Macs, you hand out whatever names you like.

**disk partition**   A **hard disk** can be partitioned
(divided) into two or more self-contained hard disks
(as seen by the computer). This helps large disks to
work more efficiently. Each partition can be run by a
different **operating system**.

**display**   A colloquial term for **monitor**.

**docking station**   A cabinet containing equipment
that extends the capabilities of a **portable computer**,
such as a larger screen, full-size keyboard and proper
mouse. The portable slides into the cabinet and
effectively becomes a **desktop computer** until it is
taken out again.

**document**   Loosely used to mean **file**, but technically
a file containing text or pictures created in a **word
processor** or **desktop publishing** program. Also used of
**Web pages**.

### domain, domain name, domain suffix

**1.** A named group of computers on a **network**,
administered as a unit, is called a domain.

**2.** Within the Internet, computers sharing a common
part of an **IP Address** are said to be in the same domain.

**3.** A domain name is the friendly name for a
**Website**, representing the user-hostile string of
numbers that is the real, unique identifier for the site.
For example, www.thetimes.co.uk and
www.apple.com are both domain names for Websites.

**4.** The domain suffix reflects the general nature or location of the Website's owner.

| Domain suffix: | Nature or location: |
| --- | --- |
| .com | commercial (for-profit) business |
| .org | non-profit organization |
| .gov | government agency |
| .edu | educational institution |
| .mil | military |
| .net | network organization |
| .uk | British |
| .de | German |

*Domain suffixes*

**DOS, DOS prompt**    DOS is the shortened form for **MS-DOS**, the predecessor of Windows. The DOS prompt (at its most basic, C:\>) is a set of characters after which the user types commands (*see* **command line**). There are still some tasks in Windows that require an expert's use of the DOS prompt.

**dot    1.** How the full stop is pronounced in **Internet addresses** and Windows and OS/2 filenames, in all of which it is used as a separator.    **2.** A dot is also the smallest element of a **bitmap**, which consists of masses of dots.

**dot-matrix printer**    A type of printer that works by pressing pins against a ribbon to create letters and numbers formed of many dots.

**dots per inch (dpi)**     Describes the quality of an image output by devices such as monitors, printers and scanners. More dots per inch equates to higher **resolution** and better quality.

**double-click**     Pressing a **mouse button** twice in quick succession. In Windows and Mac OS, double-clicking an application (program) icon will start the program, and double-clicking a file icon will open the file in the program with which it is **associated**.

**download**     To transfer a file from another computer on the Internet to your own computer. The opposite of **upload**.

**downtime**     The time during which a computer is not working, during which it is said to be 'down'. You know the feeling...

**dpi**     Acronym for **dots per inch**.

**drag, drag and drop**     To drag (move) an object on-screen, click on it to **highlight** (or **select**) it, then hold down the mouse button and move it. This drags it to another location. When used as a command, the technique is called 'drag and drop'. For example, you can drag a document onto a printer icon to print it.

**DRAM**     An older, cheaper type of **RAM**. *See also* **EDO RAM** *and* **SDRAM**.

**draw program**     Software that draws independent objects such as squares and ellipses. These are **vector graphics**, meaning that each object is stored by the computer in its own right and can be separately moved, resized and edited. Contrast with a **paint program**, in which images are stored as collections of dots. Leading examples are *Adobe Illustrator*, *Corel DRAW!* and *Macromedia Freehand*.

**driver**    A shortened form of the term **device driver**. A small program that acts as a translator between the computer and, say, a mouse or printer.

**drop-down list**    A **text box** with a drop-down arrow to its right side, found in a **dialogue box** or on a **toolbar**. Click on the arrow to drop down a list of options, from which you can choose one.

**DTP**    Acronym for **desktop publishing**.

**DVD**    Acronym for Digital Versatile Disk, a high-speed, ultra-high-capacity type of **CD-ROM**.

| 100% ▼ |
| --- |
| 500% |
| 200% |
| 150% |
| **100%** |
| 75% |
| 50% |
| 25% |
| 10% |
| Page Width |
| Whole Page |
| Two Pages |

*A drop-down list for zoom options*

# E

**e-commerce**   Buying and selling on the Internet. You'll do it one day, if you're not doing it already.

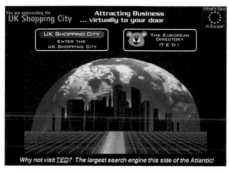

*You can now buy almost anything on the Internet*

**edit, editor**   To change **data** or **code** in any way. An 'editor' (sometimes called a 'text editor') is a program specifically designed to edit text, with negligible formatting facilities. Most commonly used is the **notepad** applet in Mac OS and Windows.

**EDO RAM**   Acronym for Extended Data Out Random Access Memory, a faster type of **DRAM**.

**edutainment** Software that is held to be both informative and entertaining. Grownups think that **infotainment** is good for them and edutainment is good for the kids.

**eject** To cause a **removable disk** (floppy disk, CD-ROM, etc.) to pop out of its drive. On a PC it's a manual process. The Macintosh has an Eject Disk command, and also ejects the disk automatically when shutting down.

**e-mail, e-mail account, e-mail address** E-mail (short for electronic mail, and sometimes spelt 'email') is a message sent via a **network** or the **Internet**, using special software such as *Outlook Express* (part of Windows 98) or *Eudora*. An **attached file** (such as a

Outlook Express *e-mail message*

word-processed document or graphic) can be sent with an e-mail. You are e-mail-ready once you have opened an account with your chosen **ISP** and registered your unique address.

**emoticon** (*emotion icon*) There's :-) (smile or 'smiley'), :-( (frown), :-* (kiss), ;-) (wink) and many others. In cyberspace, the range of human feelings is boiled down to a combination of characters, which save a lot of time and bandwidth.

**emulation** What happens when software written for a particular piece of hardware is tricked into believing that a different piece of hardware is just the same thing. For example, emulation allows many different printers to use Hewlett Packard's popular software. There is also software that enables a Macintosh to emulate a PC.

**encrypt, encryption** Coding data into a secret format, for security. **Decryption**, which requires a secret password, turns it back into its original form.

**End key** Moves the **cursor** to the end of a line of text. Ctrl+End moves the cursor to the end of the document. *See also* **Home key**.

**end user** You. Or anyone else who actually uses hardware or software as opposed to developing it.

**Enter key** Also called the Return, Hard Return and even Carriage Return (from typewriter days) key. In a word processor, pressing it completes a paragraph of text. In a database or spreadsheet, it moves the cursor to the next **field** or **cell**. It's also used to confirm a

**command** to the computer, just like clicking OK with the mouse.

**erase**   To remove or throw away; another word for **delete**.

**error message**   **1.** A message from the program to say you've made an error, often with some clue as to what to do about it.   **2.** A message from the computer that something is wrong. Sometimes there's a clue, but often it is cryptic.

**Esc key**   Esc means Escape. Generally, pressing this key cancels an action. It will also close an open **dialogue box** without applying any choices you have made.

**Ethernet**   A **local area network** standard for connecting computers, including Windows, Macintosh and Unix machines.

**etiquette**   Unwritten rules on how to behave when writing e-mail, particularly when it is circulated among several people, or when participating in an online **chat** session. There are three basic rules: be polite; be brief; and DON'T SHOUT (that is, don't use capitals unnecessarily). *See also* **netiquette**.

**Excel**   Microsoft's market-leading **spreadsheet** package, usually bought as an integrated part of the **Office** suite of programs.

**execute**   Jargon for 'do it' or 'run', as in 'Carry out the command' or 'Start the program'.

Derived from the .EXE **extension** in Windows program (or 'executable') files – for example, if you **double-click** CDPLAYER.EXE in the **root** Windows folder, it will start the CD-Player program.

**Exit**   A PC term, meaning 'Close this program'. The punchier Mac equivalent is **Quit**.

**expand**   **1.** In a Windows Explorer **folder tree**, the opposite of **collapse**: what you do when you show the contents of a folder or subfolder.   **2.** To add extra features to a computer (*see also next entry*).

**expansion bus, expansion board/card, expansion slot**   If you opted to buy a budget-level computer, you may find it has fewer features than you hoped for. You can expand it by adding extra features, such as an internal **modem** or a **sound card**. Expansion boards or cards that add these features plug into an expansion slot (of which there should be several) in the system's **motherboard**. (They are also called **adaptor** cards.) The expansion bus (also called the **I/O** bus) carries information to and from these new devices.

*Inserting an expansion card into a slot*

**export** To create a file in one program that another program understands, so allowing them both to share one set of data. For example, the *Access* database program can export tables to the *Excel* spreadsheet program. It can also **import** data from *Excel*.

**extension** **1.** A filename suffix consisting of a dot followed by up to three characters, representing the program that Windows will **associate** with the file. Thus

| Extension | File format |
|-----------|-------------|
| .123 | Lotus 1-2-3 (spreadsheet) |
| .BMP | bitmap image (graphic) |
| .COM | MS-DOS application (program) |
| .DOC | Word document (word processor) |
| .EXE | executable file (program) |
| .GIF | Graphics Interchange Format (graphic) |
| .JPG | JPEG file (graphic) |
| .LWP | WordPro document (word processor) |
| .MP3 | online music (from the Internet) |
| .NSF | Lotus Notes (groupware) |
| .RTF | Rich Text Format (formatted text) |
| .TIF | TIFF file (graphic) |
| .TTF | TrueType (font file) |
| .TXT | text file (plain, unformatted text) |
| .WPD | WordPerfect document (word processor) |
| .XLS | Excel worksheet (spreadsheet) |
| .ZIP | compressed file |

*Common Windows file extensions*

files with a .MNY suffix are associated with Microsoft *Money*, and those with .WPD with *WordPerfect*.

**2.** A small program, such as a **screen saver**, kept in the Macintosh **System Folder**, which is loaded whenever the system is started. You can add these yourself.

**external drive**    A separate box, connected to the computer by a cable and housing a **removable disk**, such as a **Zip drive**. On PCs, some can be connected directly to the **parallel port**, and on Macs, to the **SCSI** port. Others will need an **expansion card**.

# F

**FAQ**    Found on **Websites** and **newsgroups**, an acronym for Frequently Asked Questions, meaning a list of questions and answers about a topic. This prevents the same questions being asked repeatedly by newcomers to the site. Also found in information files and manuals that come with software.

**Favorites**    Microsoft's term for **bookmarks** in their **Internet Explorer** browser: marking a **Website** or **Web page** for revisiting later.

**fax modem**    The ability to send and receive faxes was once a special feature, but nowadays all modems are fax modems. However, they won't handle faxes when connected to the Internet, so if you plan to be online frequently, you may prefer to have a dedicated fax machine.

**fax software**    A program that sends and receives

*A fax cover sheet*

faxes through a **fax modem**. As in e-mail, an **attached file** such as a spreadsheet can be sent with a fax. Incoming faxes are stored electronically for you to view later.

**female connector**    One half of a connection: the receptacle on a device or cable that accepts the pins of its matching **male connector**.

**field**    **1.** A blank space in a **database**, which you fill in. They are usually arranged in vertical columns, each one recording a specific unit of information, such as people's ages or car registrations. A horizontal row of related fields makes up a **record**. The **spreadsheet** equivalent is a **cell**.    **2.** A specified location in a word-processed document into which information from a database is inserted during a **mail merge** operation.

**file, filename**    **1.** A unit of information stored on a computer, each file has its own filename, which the computer will **associate** with a particular program. A file contains either a **program** or **data**. Files are organized into **folders**.    **2.** Each program has a File **menu**, which allows you to create and store new files or open an existing one.

**file attribute**    The **operating system** holds information about the 'attributes' of each **file**. For example, it will know whether an essential system file should be hidden to prevent your deleting it. Or a file containing a legal document may be **read-only** so that it cannot be overwritten.

**file compression**    *See* **compression**.

**file conversion**    To convert or translate a file created in one program into a form (or **format**) understood by another program. For example, *Word* and *WordPerfect* can exchange data through file conversion. Special file-conversion programs are available to convert files to and from a wide range of formats. *See also* **import** *and* **export**.

**file server**    The heart of any **network** is the file server – or several of them. The file server stores all the network users' data on its own hard disk, allowing **file sharing** and swift transfers of data directly from any **workstation**. In smaller networks, all the programs used by the network may also be run from the server, and **backups**, **e-mail** traffic and connections to the Internet may also be handled through the server.

**file sharing**    A feature allowing information to be shared between computers connected to a network. The person controlling a **folder** tells the computer on which it is stored

*The Windows 95/98 Sharing dialogue box*

(usually the **file server**) that it is 'shared'. Then other users can access files in the folder too.

**file size**   How much disk space a file needs, measured in **kilobytes** or even **megabytes**. All disks, from the humble floppy upwards, have finite capacity, so file size will often be a significant issue. The size of an **attached file** sent with an e-mail is also important: the smaller, the better.

**find, find and replace**   Most programs allow you to 'find' or search for a word, phrase or fragment of text. You can also 'find and replace' it with something else, either replacing each instance, or not, as you choose, or replacing all instances throughout the document. Some programs call this 'search and replace' and others 'find and change'.

*Word 97's Find and Replace dialogue box*

**Finder**   The official name for the **desktop** on a Macintosh.

**firewall**    An appropriately lurid term for protection of networks connected to the Internet. Provided by special hardware, software or a mixture of both, a firewall protects the network from **hackers**, data theft and other perils. It checks that, for example, incoming e-mail and Web-page traffic meets security criteria set up for the **network**.

**FireWire**    A high-speed connection allowing up to 63 **devices** to connect in a 'daisy chain' to one computer. Supported by Windows 98 and Mac OS 8.5 and 9.

**fixed disk**    Another term for **hard disk**.

**flame, flame wars**    An angry, insulting message sent electronically is a 'flame'. 'Flame wars' are exchanges of furious electronic messages, sometimes witnessed publicly in Internet **newsgroups** or online **chat** areas.

**Flash**    Macromedia's *Flash* is the dominant standard for creating animated graphics on the Web, while keeping file sizes small enough for normal modem connections.

**flash memory**    A form of memory that can easily be updated through software, instead of having to replace an entire memory chip.

**flatbed scanner**    A type of **scanner** rather like a photocopier, with a sheet of glass on which you lay the image to be scanned. An additional option for flatbeds is an automatic document feeder (ADF), which automates the feeding of multiple sheets of paper when using **OCR** (text-scanning) software.

**flat panel display**    The sort of thin, flat monitor seen on a **notebook computer**. For full-size computers they are the shape of things to come, but currently cost far more than traditional TV-shaped monitors, though prices are expected to come down.

**floating toolbar**    A collection of **icons** representing software **tools**, grouped in a small movable window, which you can park wherever you like on-screen. Typically found in graphics, DTP and presentation programs.

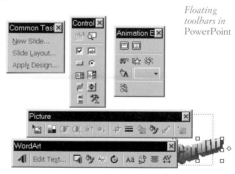

*Floating toolbars in* PowerPoint

**floppy disk, floppy disk drive (FDD)**    A removable disk encased in a 3½ inch plastic case, which, at a meagre but low-cost 1.44 megabytes, has been the standard size for many years. It is not actually at all floppy, although its 5¼ inch and 8 inch predecessors were. Pretty well all computers (though notably not the Apple **iMac**) have a slot on the front called a floppy disk drive (FDD), into which floppies are inserted. *See also* **A:**

**folder**    Space on a disk is divided by the user into storage areas, called folders. Not only do they sound like traditional cardboard folders: they also look like them, both in the Mac OS and in Windows.

**folder tree**    In **Windows Explorer**, the contents of a disk are laid out visually in a 'tree'. **Subfolders** branch out from their parent **folders**, with sub-subfolders branching out still further. You **expand** a folder (view its subfolders) or subfolder by clicking on the plus sign beside it, or **collapse** it (hide its subfolders) by clicking on a minus sign.

```
My Computer
├─ 3½ Floppy (A:)
├─ FISHTANK (C:)
│  ├─ CHP WEBSITE
│  ├─ CuteFTP
│  ├─ Display Driver S3
│  ├─ Eudora
│  ├─ Install
│  ├─ Kai's Power Goo
│  ├─ Multimedia Files
│  ├─ My Documents
│  │  ├─ Family
│  │  ├─ Finances
│  │  └─ Letters
│  ├─ Orb
│  ├─ PQMAGIC
│  ├─ Program Files
│  ├─ PSFONTS
│  │  ├─ PFM
│  │  └─ RegFiles
│  └─ RECYCLED
```

**font**    Although traditionally 'font' means a specific size and style of **typeface** (like 12-point italic Arial), in modern computers it refers simply to the whole typeface (as in Arial itself). **TrueType** fonts, supplied free with Windows PCs and Macs, provide a wide choice of high-quality

*A folder tree, showing several expanded folders*

fonts in any size, for both on-screen display and printing. The rival **PostScript** font system costs money but is widely used in professional publishing.

**footer**   An area at the bottom of each printed page reserved for document details such as page numbering, the date or the **filename**. Once set up properly in a document, the software you are using will handle these automatically.

**foreground**   On a **multitasking** computer, only the current task you are working on is in the foreground. All others are in the **background**. To put it another way, only one **window** (the one running the current task) is in the foreground (or is **active**). All other open windows are in the background.

**format, formatting**   **1.** The characteristics of an object, for example a paragraph of tont or a graphic, on the screen. You **select** (highlight) it to change its format, such as its size, appearance or position.   **2.** The command to prepare a **disk** for use by a particular **operating system**, which involves wiping it completely clean.

**formula**   In a **spreadsheet**, a calculation based on the values of two or more cells. It is worthwhile making the modest effort to master the basic formulae (addition, multiplication, etc.), because this will unleash much of the spreadsheet's potential usefulness.

**Forward button**   An on-screen **button** displayed in **Web browser** software that is used to redisplay a **Web page** you have just backed off from (using the reverse

**Back button**). In Windows 98, **Windows Explorer** also features a Forward button.

**forward slash** The / (oblique stroke) key on your keyboard is referred to as the 'forward slash'. It is used as a separator in **URLs** (or **Internet addresses**) and directories in **Unix**.

**fragmentation** To use disk space efficiently, some operating systems naturally split files into fragments, filling in spaces left when files were previously deleted. However, over time, disks become heavily fragmented, and it takes progressively longer to assemble files. The solution is to **defragment** your disk regularly.

**frame** A rectangular area used in **Web browser**, **DTP** and word-processing software to contain an independent unit of text or graphics. Each frame can be

*A three-frame Web page. Each frame can be scrolled independently*

scrolled and manipulated separately, and one page can contain several frames.

**free space**    The amount of unused space available on a disk.

**freeware**    Copyrighted software you can use free of charge. Freeware can be downloaded from the Internet or copied from a sampler CD-ROM. Compare with **public domain** software and **shareware**.

**freeze, frozen**    Short for **system freeze**, another term for **crash**: when a computer stops in its tracks and won't budge.

**FTP**    Acronym for File Transfer Protocol, a method of transferring files over the Internet now largely supplanted by the more convenient method of sending **attached files** with e-mail. But e-mail is unsuitable for handling large file attachments, so **FTP** still has its place.

**function keys**    The row of keys across the top of the keyboard, labelled F1, F2, etc. They provide **shortcuts** to various software features, which vary from one program to another. Often used in combination with the **modifier keys**. Sometimes called Fkeys, on the Macintosh.

# G

**game adaptor, game port** An **adaptor** that adds a port for connecting a **joystick** or other game control device. Standard equipment on most new computers.

**gateway** A link that enables two different kinds of **network** to connect and talk to one another. The gateway might be **LAN**-to-LAN, or LAN-to-Internet.

**GB** Short for **gigabyte**.

**gender bender, gender changer** Turns a **male connector** into a **female connector** and vice versa.

**GIF** Acronym for Graphics Interchange Format, pronounced 'jif'. A standard for storing **graphics** for all computers to use. GIF files are ideal for **Web page** graphics because of their small file size.

**gig, gigabyte** 'Gig' is slang for gigabyte, or just over one billion **bytes**.

**grammar checker** A **word processor** feature that checks your text against a set of grammar rules and then highlights any violations. It will also suggest corrections. A boon for the semi-literate, but it will infuriate the educated stylist. It can be turned off.

**graphics, graphics software** **1.** Anything pictorial – that is, non-text and non-numeric – on a computer. **2.** 'Graphics' also refers to a computer's capability for displaying and manipulating pictures – as in: 'Early

Courtly love was not only the subject of lyrics, but of long – very long – stories in prose and verse. And this reminds me of something else that the Gothic centuries added to the European consciousness: that cluster of ideas and sentiments which surround the words 'romantic' and 'romance'. One can't put it more precisely than this, because it is in the nature of romanticism to evade definition. One can't even say that romance was a Gothic invention: I suppose that, as the word suggests, it was really Romanesque, and grew up in those southern districts of France where the memories of Roman civilisation had not been quite obliterated when they were overlaid by the more fantastic imagery of the Saracens.

**Spelling and Grammar: English (British)** ? X

Long Sentence:

civilisation had not been quite obliterated when they were overlaid by the more fantastic imagery of the Saracens.

Ignore
Ignore All
Next Sentence

Suggestions:

Long Sentence (no suggestions)

Change

☑ Check grammar   Options...   Undo   Cancel

*Word's grammar checker has a problem with Kenneth Clark's Civilisation!*

computers had no graphics.'   **3.** Graphics software includes any type of program for creating and manipulating pictures, both alone and combined with text.

**graphics card**   The computer controls the monitor through its on-board graphics card, now usually integrated into the **motherboard**. The cable from the monitor plugs into it.

**greyed out**   A greyed-out **menu** command or **dialogue box** option cannot be used. You will often see the term spelled the American way, 'grayed out'. Also referred to as **dimmed.**

**greyscale**   An image in shades of grey ranging from pure black to white, allowing shadows and shapes to be depicted more realistically than in black and white only. Also used by some printers, scanners and portable computers that cannot handle colour.

*A greyscale image*

**groupware**   Software that helps groups of colleagues in a **local area network** to organize their activities. It includes e-mail, a shared **address book**, **file sharing**, a communal calendar, and other useful tools. Leading examples are *Lotus Notes* and *Microsoft Outlook*.

**guestbook**   An interactive place on a Website where visitors can leave opinions and impressions – just like a hotel guestbook.

**GUI**   (pronounced 'gooey') Acronym for Graphical User Interface. The user-friendly visual interface with a computer, via buttons, icons and other pictures, popularized by the Macintosh and, later, Windows. All applications running on a particular GUI have similar user interfaces, making it relatively easy to learn new programs.

# H

**hack, hacker**   The hacker, an unwelcome expert visitor, hacks (breaks) into a network via a modem, usually to tamper with stuff for the fun of it, but sometimes to steal data or cause malicious damage. A **firewall** provides defence.

**halftone**   A black and white image prepared for printing. Photographs need to be converted into halftones before they are scanned, otherwise many of the details would appear as blotches.

**hand-held computer**   Although small enough to be carried in one hand, they have not so far replaced **notebook computers**, and seem best suited to the personal information manager (PIM) role. Some have small keyboards, while others use a **pen** or **stylus** to enter data. Also called palmtop computer.

**handles**   Click on an object such as a graphic or **frame**, and 'handles' (small black squares) will appear at the corners and sides. Click and drag on a handle, to resize the

*You can manipulate graphics by using the handles*

object. Click inside the object and drag, to move the whole thing.

**handshake**    **1.** Two networked computers exchanging signals to indicate that they are ready to transmit data. **2.** Two modems exchanging signals before they start talking: the noise they make is the handshake taking place.

**hard copy**    A printout of data on paper is the hard copy. A computer file containing the data electronically is the **soft copy**.

**hard disk, hard disk drive**    The hard disk is a sandwich of magnetic storage plates encased in a hard disk drive (HDD), which sits inside the computer. The hard disk (often shortened to HD) is the computer's main storage device, holding the files for the **operating system**, plus the **program** and **data** files.

**hard return**    In text, what you put in when you press the **Enter key**, namely the end of a paragraph, so that the **cursor** jumps to the next line. Contrast with **soft return**. The hard-return character (¶) on-screen can be made visible or invisible.

**hardware**    The computer itself and its interior components, plus any device connected to it. To sum everything up: **software** runs on hardware.

**header**    An area at the top of each printed page reserved for document details such as page numbers, titles and subtitles. Once set up properly in a document, the software you are using will handle these automatically.

**Help, Help system**   Indexed information about how to do anything – in theory – on or with a computer, plus useful background commentary, definitions and links to related topics. Provided within all programs and operating systems, often with supplementary information available from the Web, but nowadays only rarely in printed manuals. Many operating systems now have 'Interactive Help', with step-by-step tutorials.

*A Help topic in Windows 95/98*

**highlight**   A term interchangeable with **select** and **swipe**.

**History list**   A list of previously visited sites on the Internet. In Internet Explorer, click on the History button and choose one of the timespans offered. You can return to a site by clicking on its name in the History list. Netscape Navigator has a similar facility, though less easily accessible.

**Home key**    Moves the **cursor** to the beginning of a line of text. Ctrl+Home moves to the start of the document. *See also* **End key**.

**home page**    The main page for a **Website**, from which you connect to other pages on the site. Your own home page is the first page your **Web browser** opens when it connects to the Internet: you can choose this and set it up to do what you want.

**host**    **1.** The computer you connect to when you access the Internet (known as your **ISP**'s host computer).    **2.** Any computer you connect to via a modem. Yours will be the **remote** terminal. If someone else connects to you, it's vice versa.    **3.** Any computer that provides services to others on a **network**, such as data, or access to a printer.

**hot key**    A key sequence that carries out common commands. In Windows, for example, Ctrl+S will save the current file, and repeated use of Alt+Tab will switch between all open programs. In Mac OS, Command+P opens the printer dialogue box. Hot keys can be defined (set up) by the user.

**hot link**    Data shared between two files, which can be in different programs, such that changes in one are also made in the other. A spreadsheet might be hot-linked to an excerpt in a word-processed document, so that when the main spreadsheet is changed, so too is the excerpt.

**hot spot**    An area on the screen that activates something when you click on it. In a **multimedia** document, it might run a video or play a sound. In a

Web page, a hot spot (or **hyperlink**) might jump to a linked Web page.

**hourglass icon**    What Windows shows (usually briefly) to say: 'I'm busy,' 'I'm thinking,' or just 'Bear with me.' There are no nuances, just an hourglass. The Mac shows a clockface instead of an hourglass.

**HTML**    Acronym for HyperText Markup Language, the standard code for creating **Web pages**. **Web browser** software converts the code into the colourful pages we see on the World Wide Web. *See also* **Web authoring**.

```
<html>
<head>
<title>The title of the web page goes here</title>
</head>

<body><font face="Arial">

<h1>Heading Size 1</h1>
<h2>Heading Size 2 (Smaller)</h2>

<p>Text can appear in <b>bold</b> or in <i>italic</i> or even in a
<font color="#FF0000">different colour</font>.

<p><center>This will centre text on the page.</center>

<p>Links to other pages are set out like this:
<a href="contact.html">contact details</a>.

<br><br><hr>
</font>
</body>
</html>
```

*A page of HTML*

**http://, https://**    The 'http://' prefix on most **URLs** (Web page addresses) tells the **Web browser** that it is looking at a Web page. It stands for HyperText Transfer

Protocol, meaning that it holds **HTML** information. The 's' in 'https://' means that the address is a secure Website for sending and receiving **encrypted** data, for example in e-commerce.

**hub** A connection point for computers and devices on a **local area network**, which passes data between them.

**hung** When a program has hung, it has stopped responding. With luck, you'll be able to close and restart it. If the computer has hung, you'll have to **reboot** it. Interchangeable with **crash** (or **freeze**).

**hyperlink** A longer-established term for **hot spot**, an area on the screen that activates something when you

*Click on the blue hyperlinks to jump to related articles. The WebLink button is a hyperlink to a related Website*

click on it. It originally referred only to a text link: if you are online, for example, you can click on a coloured **Internet address** in a *Word* document or e-mail to jump to the linked Web page.

**hypertext**   An electronic document through which readers plot their own paths, reading by context and association rather than in linear fashion. An article about John Lennon might lead you to a sound clip from the song 'Imagine', then on to an article on Yoko Ono's art. Ideal for **multimedia** encyclopaedias, this process is called **browsing**. The **World Wide Web** is a global hypertext system.

# I

**IBM**   In the days of **mainframes**, IBM (International Business Machines) ruled the computing world. Having then set the standard for personal computers, it lost its commercial lead through a succession of misjudged decisions, but remains the world's largest computer company, with over 40,000 well-regarded hardware and software products.

**IBM PC, IBM-compatible**   IBM's first personal computer was called the IBM PC and set the somewhat loose standard for all machines running the **MS-DOS** and, later, **Windows** operating systems. Hence the term 'IBM-compatible': broadly speaking they all work in the same way, and they all run the same software.

**icon**   A small picture that represents an object on a **GUI**-based computer: a disk, feature, program, folder or file. Icons can be moved, grouped, opened, closed,

*Icons: (left) Windows, (right) Mac OS*

**maximized** or **minimized** – providing, in other words, a key to operating the whole machine.

**IDE**   Acronym for Integrated Drive Electronics (or, depending on which expert you consult, Intelligent Device Electronics), a widely used interface between a **disk drive** and its computer. Vies with **SCSI**: your computer will very likely have one or other of them.

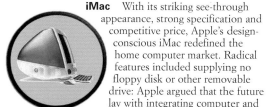

**iMac**   With its striking see-through appearance, strong specification and competitive price, Apple's design-conscious iMac redefined the home computer market. Radical features included supplying no floppy disk or other removable drive: Apple argued that the future lay with integrating computer and Internet.

*The Apple iMac*

**image-editing software**   Any program used to edit and modify **graphics** files, in particular **bitmap** files.

**import**   To take information into a program from a completely different program, for example from a spreadsheet into a database, or from one word processor into another. *See also* **export**.

**inbox**   Newly received e-mail messages are displayed in the e-mail program's folder known as the inbox.

**information superhighway**   A 'sound-bite' coined by US Vice-President Al Gore in 1993, comparing the fast-growing Internet to the US highway system. It has

come to mean the Internet itself – some would say an idealized version.

**infotainment**   Information + Entertainment. For the children's version, *see* **edutainment**.

**initialize**   **1.** To start up hardware or software, a process that involves clearing it of any old data still stored in it.   **2.** Another word for **format**, meaning to prepare a disk for use by the **operating system**, which involves wiping it completely clean.

**inkjet printer**   A type of printer that works by spraying ink in tiny dots, combining colours or using black ink. Not as good as **laser printers** for high-quality text, but far cheaper for colour work, the better models are capable of impressive results if the correct paper is used.

**input**   Anything that goes into a computer for processing, from whatever source, mechanical or

*The Insert menu in Word 97*

human. A human entering data is sometimes said to be 'inputting'.

**Insert** A **menu** that provides access to various things you can insert into a document, depending on the program you are running. It might be a new page, or a picture, or text from another file.

**insertion point** A blinking vertical cursor that indicates where the next text you type will appear.

**Insert key, insert mode** In word processing, the Insert key switches between 'insert mode' (where any new text you type will push any existing text to the right) and **overtype mode**. Millions of keyboard-fixating two-finger typists wish that the too-easily-pressed Insert key had disappeared along with the electronic typewriter.

**install** To copy **program** files onto your hard disk so that the **operating system** can find and use them. Windows uses the word **setup** to mean the same thing.

**integrated software** A set of programs designed to work effectively with each other, covering most mainstream professional needs. Alternatively called an office suite, they may include a word processor, e-mail,

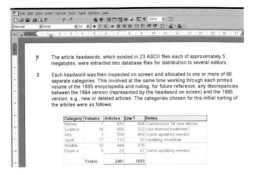

*Integrated software in action: an* Excel *worksheet inserted into a* Word *document*

spreadsheet and other programs. *Microsoft Office* for both PC and Mac is the market leader. Other effective PC options are *Corel WordPerfect Office* and *Lotus Smartsuite*. For the Mac, *AppleWorks* is a good option. *Microsoft Works* is geared towards PC home users.

**Intel**   The world's leading designer and manufacturer of **microprocessors**, notably the Pentium range of chips found in most of the world's PCs.

**IntelliMouse**   A mouse manufactured by Microsoft, with a wheel between the two buttons. Turn the wheel to scroll through documents (much easier than with a mouse); press it to access other features.

**interactive**   A computer or program that responds to you is 'interactive'. Using it is a dialogue between human and machine. Interactivity is now the norm, but 20 years ago a computer would have given you little or nothing back.

**interface**   Any point of connection between computer and user. The monitor and keyboard are interfaces. The **GUI** operating system that runs the system is a software interface. **Voice recognition** software provides a particularly direct interface.

**internal speaker**   A small speaker is built into every computer, but don't expect to hear much from it. The machine's impressive sound capabilities are only revealed by connecting external speakers and using audio software (*see* **CD Player**).

**Internet**   A worldwide network of computers, all sending, receiving or storing information. Access is provided through large companies, universities, government and military agencies, and, for individuals, through **Internet service providers**. A **Web browser** and other special software is needed to access the information held on other computers linked to the Internet. *See also* **World Wide Web**.

**Internet address**   Every computer connected to the Internet is allocated a unique number. This is its Internet address. Usually a unique name is also allocated, because names are more user-friendly than long numbers. To access an Internet address, simply type the name or number into your **Web browser**. The browser will pass it on to an Internet **gateway**, and moments later you should be online.

| Address | 🔗 http://www.pretenders.org |

*A simple Internet address*

**Internet café**    A place to drink coffee while surfing the Web or picking up your e-mail. Good too for getting a first taste of the Internet, as friendly advice and help will usually be available. Found in towns and cities all over the world.

**Internet Explorer**    A leading **Web browser** from Microsoft. Controversially, though usefully, it is integrated into Windows 98 and Windows 2000.

**Internet service provider (ISP)**    A company that provides connections to the Internet. You will need an account with at least one ISP. Price levels and quality of service fluctuate constantly in the ferociously competitive ISP market, so shop around. Prominent among the myriad choices are AOL, and its subsidiary CompuServe, Freeserve and MSN.

**Internet software**    Any software that allows you to access and use the **Internet**. Examples are **Web browser**, **e-mail** and **FTP** software.

**intranet**    A small version of the Internet contained within a **local area network**, but in every respect resembling the real thing. Information is presented in **Web page** form.

**invalid**   If your computer says that something is 'invalid', it means it is incorrect or unexpected.

**I/O**   Stands for Input/Output, the computer's most basic operation.

**IP, IP Address**   IP stands for Internet Protocol, the method of sending information around the Internet. An IP Address is specifically the string of numbers that is each computer's unique **Internet address**, which locates it on the Net. Normally what you use is the more memorable verbal form of the address.

**IRC**   Acronym for Internet Relay Chat. Most people just call it **chat**.

**ISDN**   Acronym for Integrated Services Digital Network, a high-capacity phone-line service much used by businesses, and some home users, for Internet connections. Cheaper, faster solutions are already starting to displace it, principally ADSL (Asymmetric Digital Subscriber Line), which does not require new wiring.

**ISP**   The acronym (and the usual term) for **Internet service provider**. Plural: ISPs, pronounced 'aye ess pees'.

**italic**   A form of **typeface** in which text prints *slanted* (italicized).

# J

**jack**   A hole in the back of a computer into which you plug an appropriate connector.

**Java**   A programming language developed by Sun Microsystems allowing programs to run on any system.

**Java applet**   A small, easily downloaded **Java** program. For example, a Java applet might be inserted into a Web Page to run an interaction animation.

**JavaScript**   A scripting language (simple programming language) developed by Netscape, which allows Web designers to incorporate advanced interactive features. Anyone can use it as it is an 'open language'.

**Jaz disk, Jaz drive**
A fast, high-capacity **removable disk** manufactured by Iomega, with a capacity of up to 2 **gigabytes**, and therefore very suitable for **backups**. Jaz drives can be either internal or external.

**joystick**   A device used for game-playing, and particularly for flight simulators. Just like a joystick in an aeroplane cockpit, you move a handle around to control where you want to go on-screen.

**JPEG**  A graphic file format that is much smaller than the **GIF** format, so ideal for Web graphics, although not always the best solution technically. JPEG files have a .JPG **extension**. JPEG (pronounced 'jay peg') stands for Joint Photographic Experts Group.

**justify**  *See* **alignment**.

# K

**K, Kb, KB**   K and KB are both abbreviations of **kilobyte**. Kb is short for **kilobit**.

**kerning**   Adjusting the spacing between letters so that they look good, in a DTP or word-processing program.

Depending on the **typeface**, certain letters look better closer or farther apart. Many fonts kern automatically.

*Kerning: before (left) and after (right)*

**key**   **1.** A button on a keyboard.   **2.** A special code or keyword needed to **encrypt** or **decrypt** a file. **3.** A criterion you use when searching in a database – *see* **query**.

**keyboard**   The keyboard is still the serious way to talk to your computer, **voice-recognition** software notwithstanding. One day, like *Star Trek*, we'll just say, 'Tea, Earl Grey, one sugar.'

**Key Caps**   A Macintosh program, found in the **Apple menu**, which appears as a small keyboard on-screen. It shows the characters produced by typing different combinations of keystrokes, for any typeface you can select on the system. The Windows equivalent is Character Map, found in Accessories, System Tools.

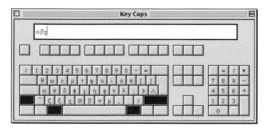

*Key Caps displaying the symbol font*

**keypad**    Either of the conveniently placed groups of keys on the right of the **keyboard**: the **cursor keys** (which include the **arrow keys**) and the **numeric keypad**.

**keyword**    The text you enter in a **find** or **search** command in a word processor, Web browser or other program.

**kill**    To **delete** or erase a file.

**kilobit, kilobyte**    A kilobit (Kb) is 1,024 **bits**; the term is mainly used about computer memory chips. The more familiar kilobyte (K or KB) equals 1,024 **bytes** ($2^{10}$, hence the extra 24) and is used as a measure of disk storage capacity. This tends to be rounded down to 1,000 bytes to make things easier, especially when referring to the speeds at which **modems** transmit data.

# L

**LAN** Acronym for **Local Area Network**.

**landscape orientation** An option in a print dialogue box, which turns a page on its side so that the long edge is at the top – like a landscape painting. Contrast with **portrait orientation**.

*Orientation: landscape (far left) and portrait*

**language** Short for **programming language**.

**laptop computer** A **portable computer** small enough to sit on your lap. Also known as a **notebook computer**.

**laser printer** A type of printer that uses a laser beam to generate an image by charging a photostatic drum with **toner**. The image is then transferred by the rotating drum to paper. The fast speed and high **resolution** of laser printers balance their higher cost and larger size, although for colour work they are expensive. A **PostScript** laser printer will provide precise typographic output.

**launch**   To **load**, **run** or start a program.

**LCD**   Abbreviation of liquid crystal display, the type of monitor used for portable computers. Flat, slim and less power-hungry than conventional monitors, they are starting to become affordable for desktop use too.

*LCD monitor*

**leading**   The vertical space between lines of text. Before electronic printing, the space was made with thin strips of lead.

**link**   **1.** Short for **hot link**, where data changed in one file automatically updates the same data in another file.   **2.** Also short for **hyperlink**, where a bit of text or a graphic on a Web page accesses something else on the Internet when you click on it.

**Linux**   A free operating system that is a close adaptation of **Unix**. Usable on many platforms, including PCs and Macintoshes, it has achieved something of a cult status as an alternative to Microsoft's ubiquitous Windows.

**liquid crystal display**   *See* **LCD**.

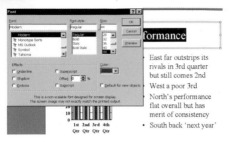

*List boxes in* PowerPoint

**list box**   A list of choices within a **dialogue box**, often large enough to require **scrolling**.

**lite**   A low-cost version of a program, lacking certain features but still usable. Occasionally spelled 'light'.

**load**   **1.** After you start a program, it is 'loaded', or transferred, from the hard disk into the computer's **RAM** (memory).   **2.** An alternative term for the **open** command.

**local area network (LAN)**   A group of computers connected together, usually in one location, so that they can share information and other resources provided by a dedicated **server**, such as printing, backups and Internet access. Usually referred to by its acronym, LAN.

**LocalTalk**   The cables and connectors that link Macintosh computers in an **AppleTalk** network.

**log in/on, log off** A similar process is involved in logging in – or on – to either a **local area network** or to the Internet through your **ISP**. Your computer sends your **user name** and **password** to the server on which you have an **account**. The server verifies these and then connects you. Logging off tells the server to terminate the connection, which otherwise would remain open as long as your machine was running.

**login name** More usually called **user name**.

**Lotus** The software company responsible for two pioneering and still popular packages, the *Lotus 1-2-3* **spreadsheet** and *Lotus Notes* **groupware** programs. *Lotus Smartsuite* is an example of **integrated software**. Now part of the giant **IBM** company.

**lowercase** ...if it isn't **UPPERCASE** then it's lowercase.

**LPT port** What PCs call the **parallel port** or **printer port**. The first – and often only – one is designated

*Connecting to the LPT port*

LPT1 and is usually what you should point your printer at when setting it up.

**lurk, lurker**    Lurkers read messages in an Internet **newsgroup** but post none themselves.

# M

**M, Mb, MB**  M and MB are both abbreviations of **megabyte**. Mb is short for **megabit**.

**Mac**  The short, familiar name for the **Macintosh** computer.

**machine language**  The actual language spoken by computers, kept well out of sight of most human beings and written entirely in numbers.

**Macintosh**  Apple's Macintosh (or **Mac**), launched in

*The Mac OS look*

1984, was one of the earliest personal computers and has long been the main rival to the **IBM-compatible** platform. It is the market leader in some important sectors, such as design, graphics and DTP. *See also* **Mac OS**, **iMac** *and* **Power Macintosh**.

**Mac OS**    Apple's **operating system** for the **Macintosh**. The earliest versions popularized the windows-and-icon-based **GUI** as the standard interface between computer and operator.

**macro**    A 'recording' of a repetitive series of commands, which can be replayed – or reused – later. Most programs allow you to create and edit macros, ranging from extremely simple to sophisticated and intricate. For example, a macro might automatically put a random list into alphabetical order, make the first entry under A, B, etc. bold and set in capitals, and insert a line space between each entry. If you then received 50 randomly sorted lists, you could process each of them like this with a single 'play the macro' command.

**magnetic disk**    A reusable, magnetically charged disk on which computer data is stored. This is the basis of the **hard disk** and **floppy disk**.

**mail**    Short for **e-mail**. In the electronic world there is no prospect of someone thinking you mean the traditional postal service.

**mail bomb**    An electronic terrorist tactic, involving orchestrating a huge amount of e-mail directed to one targeted **mailbox**. Unable to cope, the mailbox is shut down and becomes unusable.

**mailbox**    A storage area on a **mail server** is designated for every user with an account. E-mail is held there until the user retrieves any waiting messages.

**mailing list**    A group of people who exchange messages by e-mail. To distribute a message to all of them, you simply send it to the mailing list.

**mail merge**    A word processor feature that enables information from a **database** to be inserted automatically into **fields** (specified locations), to create mass mailings of personalized letters. The information inserted will include names, addresses and greeting lines. Envelopes or mailing labels can also be generated.

**mail server**    On a **local area network** or on the Internet, one computer, the mail server, sends and receives **e-mail**. Incoming mail is stored on it until retrieved by users. When you **log on** to your **ISP**, you are connecting to its mail server.

**mainframe**    Popularly associated with yesteryear's image of huge machines festooned with tape spools and

tended by white-coated boffins. But today's mainframe is a very powerful, expensive PC-like computer capable of supporting thousands of clients and many different programs simultaneously.

**male connector**   The half of a connection on a device or cable that inserts pins into a matching **female connector**.

**manual**   Rather a rarity these days, a printed document giving instructions for using hardware or software. Now frequently supplanted by the **Help system** in software form. The decline of official manuals spawned a publishing boom in 'how-to' books covering every imaginable computer-related topic.

**map, mapped**   The 'Map Network Drive' command in Windows is used to make a network connection through a server and assign it a letter. For example, after you connect (map) to a colleague's hard disk drive and give it the naming letter F: (say), you can access folders on it just like on your own hard disk. *See also* **network drive**.

*The Windows Map Network Drive dialogue box*

**margin**   The space all round the edge of a page.

**maximize, Maximize button**   To return a window to its full size, using the Maximize button. An application window (for the program you are running) will fill the entire screen. A file window (for the file you have open) will fill the available working area inside the application window. *See also* **minimize**.

**Mbps**   Acronym for **megabits** per second.

**media**   Objects used for storing computer-generated data, such as hard or floppy disks, CDs of various kinds, tape, and even paper or other printing media (as in **hard copy**).

**megabit, megabyte**   A megabit (Mb) is one million **bits**; data-transfer rates in networks are often measured in megabits per second (**Mbps**). The more familiar megabyte (M or MB), meaning 1,024 **kilobytes**, is the unit of measurement for high-capacity **media** such as hard disks. It is colloquially called a 'meg'.

**megahertz**   Abbreviated to MHz and meaning one million cycles per second. The unit of measurement for the speed of **microprocessors**, known as the **clock speed**. This determines how many instructions per second can be handled, so MHz numbers are significant.

**memory**   Memory holds working information, in the form of instructions to the computer, and data that you have entered but not yet saved. There are two types: **ROM** (Read-Only Memory), which holds permanent instructions, and **RAM** (Random-Access Memory),

*The Format menu in Word 97*

which holds transient instructions and is only active while the computer has power. Each time you save a file, the transient data is transferred permanently from RAM to disk.

**menu, menu bar**   A menu is a list of program commands grouped into related tasks. The menu drops down from the menu bar, the line across the top of the screen that holds several menus. For example, the File menu contains commands for working with the file (Open, Save, Print, Exit, etc.), and the View menu contains commands that control the view on-screen (the degree of **zoom** or size of the working area, the tools available to you, etc.).

**menu-driven**   Controlled through menus – the opposite of **command-driven**.

**message box**   A box that presents a message from the program you are running. It might be a warning, or confirmation that a task has been completed.

*An Access message box*

**MHz**   Abbreviation for **megahertz**.

**micro-**   A prefix meaning 'one millionth', which has been stuck imprecisely onto computer-related words to mean 'very small' (except in the case of Microsoft, which is very large indeed).

**microprocessor**   The **central processing unit**: the chip that controls most of what a computer does. Examples are the **PowerPC chips** made by Motorola and IBM for **Power Macintosh** computers, the **Pentium** range of chips for PCs made by **Intel**, and the rival products from AMD.

**Microsoft**   The company behind the **Windows** operating system, which runs most of the world's desktop computers (and its predecessor, **MS-DOS**, which was every bit as ubiquitous), the **Internet Explorer** browser, and MSN (Microsoft Network), the **ISP** and Web **directory**. Microsoft also publishes much of the most popular application software for PCs and

*The Intel Pentium III microprocessor*

Macs: the integrated **Office** suite, incorporating *Word*, *Excel*, *Access*, *PowerPoint* and *Outlook*; *FrontPage*, for **Web authoring**; *Publisher*, a budget-priced **desktop publishing** package; *Encarta*, a **multimedia** encyclopaedia and atlas; and several others.

**MIDI**   Acronym for Musical Instrument Digital Interface, a hardware-and-software standard for exchanging musical information between PCs and musical instruments, most typically keyboards.

**MIME**   Acronym for Multipurpose Internet Mail Extensions, a format for encoding e-mail and transferring it through the Internet. Pictures, sounds and other **attached files** can also be encoded with MIME, which is supported by many e-mail programs.

**minimize, Minimize button**   To shrink a window to an icon button on the **taskbar**, using the Minimize button. Clicking the icon button will restore the window (or **maximize** it).

**minitower computer**   A computer with an upright case, smaller than a **tower computer** and therefore small enough to stand on your desk, but also designed to go under a desk.

**mirror site**   A separate Internet site containing the same information as an original site. Often used to increase capacity for very busy Web pages. The term also covers sites that have the same content but use different languages.

**modem**   Short for MOdulator-DEModulator (though always called 'modem'), a device that converts data from

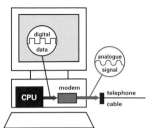

*A modem converts digital data from the CPU into an analogue signal that can be transmitted over a telephone line*

computer (**digital**) format into phone (**analogue**) format and vice versa. This enables computers to communicate with one another via phone lines.

**modifier key**   A key that combines with (or modifies) other keys to give commands to the computer. The **Alt key**, **Ctrl key** and **Shift key** are found on both PCs and Macs. The Mac additionally has the **Command key** (or **Apple key**).

**monitor**   The formal name for the bit you stare into, also known as the screen or display. The best advice when choosing a monitor: get the largest one you can afford. The best advice once you've got it: use the highest **resolution** your eyes will tolerate. The higher the resolution, the more useful stuff can be fitted onto the **desktop**.

**morphing**   The technique of blending one image smoothly into another to create radical transformations.

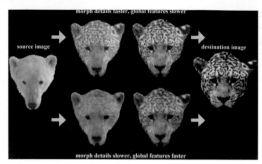

*A bear is transformed (morphed) into a big cat*

Think of *Terminator 2*. Morphing software brings such effects to the average computer.

**motherboard**   The computer's main circuit board, to which most **devices** connect. It holds the **central processing unit**, **memory** chips, **buses** and **expansion slots**. Motherboards can even sprout a supplementary daughterboard.

**mouse, mouse button, mouse pad**   The mouse (plural: mice) is a **pointing device**: you move it around on a mouse pad, and a pointer on screen imitates your hand movement. You point at items on-screen, **select** them by clicking the mouse buttons, **drag** (move) them around, and generally manipulate them.

**move**   A command that transfers what you just **selected** to a new location. For example, files can be moved to new folders, and elements of an *Excel* **worksheet** can be moved to another worksheet.

**MP3**   A tool for compressing music files to such an extent that they can be sent in bulk across the Internet and stored on a hard disk. Alternatively, more than 14 hours' play can be stored on one CD. For playback, the computer needs MP3 Player software. MP3 offers revolutionary possibilities for the future distribution of recorded music.

**MS-DOS**   Acronym for Microsoft Disk Operating System, often abbreviated to DOS. The **command-driven** operating system with which Microsoft made its reputation and early fortune, after IBM chose it to run the original **IBM PC**. Windows was originally a **GUI** for DOS, and a few experts argue that DOS is still running the real show underneath Windows.

**multimedia**   A program that combines graphics, text, sound, video and some degree of user interaction. The most popular examples are encyclopaedias.

*The* Hamlet *CD-ROM combines pictures, text, audio, and video in a multimedia study aid*

**multitask, multitasking**    A computer's ability to run several programs or tasks at the same time. Generally only one is **active**, the others being open but inactive in the **background** but available to be switched to in an instant. Such tasks as printing, **downloading** files from the Internet, or sending and receiving e-mail can also continue while you work in, say, your word processor: this is true multitasking.

**My Computer**    An icon on the Windows **desktop**, which opens a window representing the basic contents of the PC. There are icons for each **disk drive**, the CD-ROM, **network drives**, the **Control Panel**, printers and other key elements.

*The My Computer window*

**My Documents**    The **default** folder created by Windows for storing your data: all **Office** programs will assume you want to save files to My Documents unless you change the default. This arrangement is ideal for some and anathema to others, so just take control. My Documents may be ignored but should never be deleted.

# N

**navigate** To find your way around an unfamiliar computer, a new program or a complicated file; or to move around the Web.

**nerd, nerdette** Male and female versions of a computer fanatic.

**Net** Abbreviation for the **Internet**.

**Net address** Short for **Internet address**.

**netiquette**
How to behave on the Internet. Don't shout IN CAPITALS. Emphasize by enclosing words *between asterisks*. Be brief, be to the point, and be off. And be  polite, especially to **newbies**. *See also* **etiquette** (for e-mails).

**Net PC** A low-cost networked computer with no **removable disks** or upgradeable **expansion slots**. Its role is to connect to a **local area network** or the Internet, from which it obtains all its services.

**Netscape Navigator**    Once the dominant **Web browser** and still the main rival to **Internet Explorer**. Netscape is now owned by AOL, a leading Internet service provider.

**network**    A group of computers connected together, usually by cabling, and often through a dedicated **server** sharing information and other resources such as file storage, backups, printing and Internet access. This model is called a 'client-server' network. Small 'peer-to-peer' networks have no dedicated **file server**: they all share files together. A network in a single location is called a **local area network** (LAN). One spanning two or more locations is called a **wide area network** (WAN).

**network computer**    Another term for a **Net PC**.

**network drive**    A disk drive on another computer to which you have connected (or **mapped**) through a network. You can then access information on it just as if it were on your own machine.

**Network Neighborhood**    If you are in a Windows network, click on the Network Neighborhood icon to display all the shared resources you are connected to, such as folders on the **file server** and **network drives**.

**network operating system (NOS)**    A term reserved for software that includes special networking enhancements to control a **local area network**. Popular examples are *Microsoft Windows NT Server* and *Novell*

*User Manager for Domains in Windows NT Server 4.0 lists network account holders and features tools for controlling their privileges and levels of access*

*Netware*. Some **operating systems**, for example **Mac OS** and **Unix**, have built-in networking features and technically don't count as true NOSs, although they will, of course, operate a network.

**New**   The command that leads to a new, blank document.

**newbie**   Usually refers to someone new to a **newsgroup**. Occasionally, a computing novice. Either way, be patient and courteous – everyone starts as a newbie.

**newsgroup**   A discussion area on the Internet, where people sharing a common interest can exchange opinions, messages, questions and answers. Correctly called **Usenet** newsgroups. *See also* **thread**.

**notebook computer** Most **portable computers** are technically notebook computers, implying that they are the size of a (large, heavy) notebook. The commonly used term **laptop computer** strictly refers to an older generation of knee-crushing 'portables'.

**notepad** A simple, swiftly accessed, text-only word processor found on Macs and PCs, useful for writing simple notes without all the palaver of modern word processors. Ideal also as a **text editor** for programmers writing or editing computer code.

```
No_Trix.txt - Notepad                                    _ □ x
File  Edit  Search  Help
Called Notepad in Windows and Note Pad on the Macintosh, the applet has
the virtue of very few word-processing features. It's the nearest thing
to the old-fashioned typewriter you'll find on today's
all-singing-all-dancing computers. Note how in the previous sentence
Notepad did not insert a line break after the 'soft hyphen' in
'all-singing-'. It knows nothing about such refinements, nor tricks
like turning ' ' (foot symbols) into proper curly quotes.
```

*Notepad in Windows*

**numeric keypad** The calculator-style keypad to the right of the keyboard. *See also* **NumLock key**.

**NumLock key** The key that switches the dual-purpose **numeric keypad** between 'cursor mode' (for cursor movement) and 'numeric mode' (for entering numbers).

# O

**OCR**   Acronym for Optical Character Recognition software, which works with a **scanner** to read (scan) a page of text and convert it into characters that can then be edited and formatted in a word processor. Modern OCR software is capable of impressive accuracy and reasonable speed, especially when the scanner is equipped to take dozens of sheets of paper.

**Office**   Microsoft's best-selling **integrated software** package for both PCs and Macs includes *Word* (for word processing), *Excel* (spreadsheet), *Access* (database), *PowerPoint* (presentation), *Outlook* (groupware) and *FrontPage* (Web authoring), plus other programs.

**office suite**   An alternative term for **integrated software**.

**offline**   **1**. When you **download** information from the Web, then disconnect from the Internet and read the information at your leisure, you are doing so 'offline'. *See also* **online**.   **2**. A printer that is not receiving data is offline. (It should be online.)

**OK button**   Click the OK button in most **dialogue boxes** to confirm your command. Your choices will be applied and the dialogue box will close.

**online** **1.** When you are connected to the Internet, you are online. **2.** A printer is online when it is receiving data. *See also* **offline.**

**online content/service provider** Online services such as news and information are provided by for-profit companies such as AOL, CompuServe, MSN and Prodigy. Online content is mostly synonymous with online service but indicates a company that generates at least some of its own content, such as Ask Jeeves.

*AOL (America Online) is a leading online service provider*

**open**   To start a program or, once the program is
running, to open a file using the Open command,
usually found in the File menu.

**operating system (OS)**   The software that runs not
only the actual computer but also the programs.
Without an OS a computer would be almost inert. Well-
known examples are **Windows**, **MS-DOS**, **Mac OS**,
**Unix**, **Linux** and **OS/2**.

**optimize**   To make things perform at their best.
Computers and other devices, operating systems and
programs can all optionally be fine-tuned to deliver
their utmost capabilities. Some of this can be done by
any competent user, but sometimes it requires
professional input.

**option button**   Once called radio buttons, option
buttons appear in groups in **dialogue boxes**. They offer
one-only choices: you can only select one option button
in any group.

**Option key**   In the USA, the Mac's equivalent to the
**Alt key**. British Macs have a conventionally named Alt
key, but people still call it the Option key.

**OS/2**   A **GUI** operating
system for PCs developed
by IBM and Microsoft. In
an epoch-making split,
Microsoft then left the
partnership to concentrate
on Windows. IBM have
persisted, gaining gradual

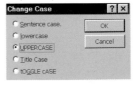

*Option buttons (Word 97)*

respect but only limited support from the market. OS/2 will run all DOS and Windows software, but not vice versa.

**outbox**   Outgoing e-mail messages are held in an e-mail program's outbox folder until you go **online** and send them.

**outline font**   A typeface that displays only the outlines of its characters, which is useful for headlines.

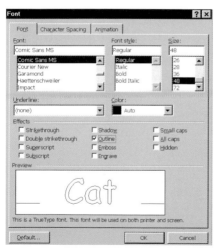

*Selecting an outline font*

Some fonts have an outline option; others were designed to be outline.

**Outlook, Outlook Express**   *Outlook* is part of Microsoft's **Office** suite and fits into the **groupware** category of software. *Outlook Express*, integrated into Windows 98 and 2000 and **Internet Explorer** 4 and 5, concentrates on online features, with advanced e-mail and **newsgroup** features.

**output**   The opposite of **input**. Everything that comes out of a computer is termed 'output', and does so via 'output devices'. This covers everything from pictures on-screen, or sound from speakers, to printed pages.

**overtype mode**   In this mode any new text you type writes over text already on-screen. Achieved by pressing the **Insert key**, which switches between overtype and **insert mode**.

# P

**page**   Each printed sheet from a program equals a page. Electronic 'pages' on computers are set up to equate to a real printed sheet, so that page starts and ends are communicated accurately to the printer.

**page break**   Where a page ends and another begins. In word processors they can be seen on-screen. Normally, if you just keep typing, the computer will 'break' (turn) pages by itself when they are full up; these are called 'soft page breaks'. If you insert additional matter anywhere, the pages will automatically be broken at new points. You can insert permanent 'hard page breaks' at any point on the page by pressing Ctrl+Enter.

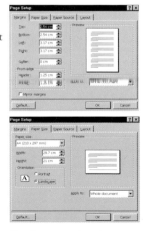

**page layout**
**1.** Anything that affects the appearance of printed pages: page size, orientation, margins, etc. Often called Page Setup by programs.   **2.** An alternative term for **desktop publishing**.

*Page layout: margin and paper size settings*

**Page Up/Page Down keys**    Generally you press these to display either the previous or the next screen of information. There are some variations between programs.

**pagination**    Splitting a long document into pages. Rather than leaving this to the computer, it is better to take control by reviewing the pagination before printing the document, making any adjustments you wish.

**paint program**    A program principally for creating and editing **bitmap graphics**, or images made up of **dots** (**pixels**). Its main tools include a brush, pen, spraycan and eraser.

Windows Paint, a standard accessory, is a very basic paint program. Professional examples include *Adobe Photoshop*, *Paint Shop Pro* and *Corel PhotoPaint*.

**palette**    A selection of colours or patterns to be applied to whatever you have selected, found in **paint programs**, **spreadsheets** and

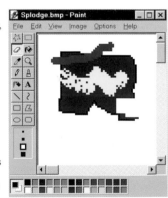

Windows Paint, *a stripped-down paint program*

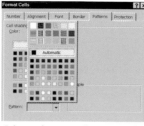

*Colour and pattern palettes in* Excel

other programs. Click a square to apply your chosen colour or pattern, or mix your own.

**palmtop computer** A fancier term for **hand-held computer**.

**pane** You can split a window in some programs and leading Web browsers into several parts or 'panes', and display different views or parts of a file in them. This can be useful for assessing complex spreadsheets or comparing portions of word-processed documents.

**parallel** Occurring simultaneously, which in computing refers to data that is transmitted more than one bit at a time ('in parallel' in other words). Most modern printers are parallel. *Compare with* **serial**.

**parallel port** PCs call it the **LPT port**, but the correct term is parallel port. Printers mostly, but also other devices, plug into it.

**partition** The act of creating a **disk partition**.

**password, password-protected** Access to anything that is password-protected requires a secret password. That can include computers themselves, networks, protected folders or files, e-mail and various kinds of Website and other resources.

**paste**    To insert information placed on the **Clipboard** by **copy** or **cut** commands.

**path, pathname**    Interchangeable terms for the location of a file on disk. It consists of the disk letter, folder, subfolders and the filename with its **extension**, all separated by **backslashes** – C:\David\Personal\ DVLC_letter.wpd is a simple example.

**PC**    Acronym for personal computer, once exclusively associated with IBM's first PC but now used of all **IBM-compatible** computers (although Macintosh computers are personal too). A PC is a complete self-contained system, capable of standalone or networked use.

**PC Card**    Credit-card-sized devices that slide into slots in a **notebook computer** to save opening the case and interfering with the compact, tightly packed circuitry. Typical uses are to add a modem, a network connection or extra RAM. Formerly called PCMCIA cards.

*An external device can be added to a notebook computer by means of a PC Card, which plugs into a slot on the side*

**PDA**    Acronym for Personal Digital Assistant, a **hand-held computer.**

**PDF**    Acronym for Portable Document Format, a file created by Adobe's *Acrobat* software. It contains text and graphics that most computers can read, using *Acrobat Reader*, which is readily available as **freeware**. Files in this format are often found on the Web.

**PDL**    Acronym for Page Description Language, a complex **programming language** that literally describes every single element of the layout and content of a page. Any printer that also understands the language can then output the page with fast and precise results. The best-known PDL is **PostScript**.

**pen, pen computing**    A pen-like **pointing device**, better described as a stylus, used with a computer equipped with a screen and software that understands what you write on the screen. Tidy, printed handwriting is the key to getting anywhere. As it is difficult for both human and machine to make good sense with pen computing, the technology has so far made rather less impact than was at one time expected.

**Pentium, Pentium Pro**    The family of **Intel** processors at the heart of most of the world's current generation of computers. The present Pentium III and even the Pentium II far outstrip the original Pentium and its successor the Pentium Pro. Built into the chip from the Pentium II onwards, Intel's MMX technology has kept it ahead of the heaviest demands made by the newest multimedia programs. AMD's

Athlon family of very fast processors offers the major competition.

**People search**  How to find someone on the Internet. There are specialized 'People search' engines, such as *Yahoo! People Search* and *Scoot*.

*Looking for someone on the Net*

**peripheral device**  Any hardware attached to the computer, whether internal (such as disk drives or the CD-ROM), integral to its operation (such as the monitor or keyboard), or external (such as a printer, mouse or modem). Often shortened to 'device'.

**personal computer**  Usually shortened to **PC**. A single-user **computer** based on a **microprocessor**, which can be linked to others to form a **network**.

**personal digital assistant** A grandiose way of saying **hand-held computer**. Sounds better abbreviated to PDA.

**personal information manager (PIM)** Software for organizing your life: a diary, address book, calendar, reminder and calculator rolled into one.

**phone jack** What you plug a phone cable into. The other end of the cable can go into a **modem**.

**Photo CD** A Kodak-developed format for storing digital photographs on CD-ROM.

**PIM** Acronym for **personal information manager**.

**piracy** Most programs are sold with a licence for a specified number of users: one, in the case of non-business customers. People who copy software without paying for it are known as software pirates.

**pixel** Abbreviation for PICture ELement, a single dot, the smallest element of a **bitmap** graphic. Monitor displays are also made up of pixels, or tiny dots of colour. An image is said to be 'pixelated' (or 'blocky', or even pixelly) if the dots stand out intrusively, as they do on older computer games.

**platform** Something on which something else 'sits' (so clearly not a railway term). An operating system sits on a microprocessor platform, and a program sits on an operating system. Most usually encountered in references to 'the Windows platform', etc.

**Plug and Play** A Windows feature that recognizes a new hardware **device** when you next start up and either sets up the necessary **driver** automatically or asks you for the disk. A breeze when it works properly (i.e. automatically).

**plug-in** A program that extends the capability of your **Web browser**, for example to play a video or music file. Some plug-ins download and install automatically.

**PNG** Acronym for Portable Network Graphics, a new licence-free format similar to **GIF** and intended to replace it as its Internet standard.

**point** **1.** What you do when you use the mouse or some other **pointing device** to move a symbol called the **pointer** to a specific object on the screen. **2.** A typographic measurement, used to measure the height of **characters**. A point is about $\frac{1}{72}$ of an inch, so a 12-point letter 'o' is about $\frac{1}{6}$ inch tall.

**pointer** The symbol on the screen that moves around when you move the mouse. It may vary between programs, and different functions within a program may also alter its appearance.

**pointing device** Anything that lets you point at a screen and move a **pointer**: a **mouse**, **pen** (or stylus), **touchpad**, or half a dozen other ingenious gadgets.

**POP3**   POP (Post Office Protocol) is the method used for retrieving e-mail by computers on the Internet. Every **ISP** has a POP3 server to which you connect to pick up your e-mail. *See also* **MIME** *and* **SMTP**.

**pop-up menu**   In Windows, a **menu** that pops up somewhere on-screen (but not down from the menu bar) when you **right-click** the mouse or press the special pop-up menu button on the keyboard. On a Mac, it is a menu that appears within a menu when you click on a down-pointing black triangle (▼); actually they pop down, not up.

**port**   A connection point (**jack**), usually in the back of a computer, into which you plug **peripheral devices** such as a printer, scanner, mouse or monitor. *See also* **parallel port**, **serial port** *and* **SCSI**.

*On a PC, select something, then right-click to get a pop-up menu such as this*

**portable computer**   This self-explanatory term covers both the **notebook computer** and **hand-held computer** genres. *See also* **docking station**.

**portrait orientation**   The option in a print dialog box that positions a page in its usual position, that is, with the narrow side at the bottom – like a portrait painting. This is the position to which the printer will

**default** unless told otherwise. *Contrast with* **landscape orientation**.

**post** **1.** To publish a message online, for example by adding it to a **newsgroup** or a **bulletin board**. **2.** To copy a new **Web page** or **Website** to a **Web server** so that other Internet users can view it.

**PostScript** Adobe's widely used page description language (*see* **PDL**) enables an accurate reproduction of a text-and-graphics layout to be printed on any PostScript-capable printer, no matter what its **resolution**. Pages perfected on-screen can be proofed to your satisfaction on your PostScript laser printer, at low resolution, and then taken to a typesetting bureau for high-resolution output on a Linotronic device. The invention of PostScript enabled **desktop publishing** to revolutionize typesetting, which was previously an expensive specialism.

**power down** To turn off your computer and any other equipment.

**Power Macintosh** A **Macintosh** based on the **PowerPC chip**, approximately equivalent to a Pentium-generation PC.

**PowerPC, PowerPC chip** The PowerPC chip, produced by Motorola and IBM, a very fast main processor that powers the current generation of Apple computers, which are referred to generically as PowerPCs. They include the **Power Macintosh** range, the **PowerBook** notebook computer series, and the popular **iMac**.

**power supply**   An internal device that converts AC power from the wall into DC power for the computer and any machines it is serving.

**power switch**   Also known as the on/off button.

**power up**   To turn on your computer and any other equipment.

**ppm**   Acronym for pages per minute, the speed at which printers do their stuff. For sheer speed, laser printers are way ahead of the rest.

**presentation software**   Also known as presentation graphics or business graphics, a type of business program for creating highly visual presentations, including charts, graphs, text, sound and even video.

*Slides in a* PowerPoint *presentation*

Microsoft's PowerPoint (part of the **Office** suite) is the best-known example.

**print**   To print information from a file, you send it to a printer by using the Print command in the File menu (or one of various shortcuts). You can print a whole file, or just one page, or a selection of pages, or even just the particular element of the file you have highlighted (**selected**) on-screen. There are other options too, some very sophisticated, depending on the program and printer you are using.

**printer**   A machine that prints text or illustrations (the printed pages are often termed the **hard copy**). For the main choices on offer, *see* **bubble-jet printer**, **dot-matrix printer**, **inkjet printer** *and* **laser printer**.

**printer font**   Printers have a limited number of 'printer fonts' stored on-board, which in a self-test they

*An inkjet printer (left) and laser printer (right)*

can actually output all by themselves, without help from any computer. One way or another, all other fonts have to be supplied to them from a computer's memory. This was

*A TrueType test page, demonstrating how one font file will support all required type sizes*

formerly a serious complication for ordinary computer users, but the advent of **TrueType** for both PCs and Macs sorted the mess out.

*Sophisticated controls for a PostScript laser printer*

**printer port**   The port through which you connect a printer to your computer. Usually the **LPT port** (or **parallel port**) on a PC.

**print job**   Sitting in the **print queue** waiting to be printed.

**print preview**   A feature that lets you see exactly how your file will look when printed, so you can make last-minute changes to **page breaks**, **margins**, etc. Of perhaps limited usefulness in a modern word processor, where your work on-screen is identical to how it looks when printed. But 'print preview' is an essential tool in applications like spreadsheets, where the graphical display is geared more towards functionality than final appearance.

**print queue**    More than one document waiting to be printed involves a queue, particularly where a printer is shared on a network. This is an orderly, if sometimes slow, process taken care of by the computer supporting the printer.

**Print Screen key**    Many computer users do not know about this hidden treasure. Press Print Screen to copy an image of what's on the screen to the **Clipboard**. Then paste the image into your word processor or **paint program**. Useful for capturing **error messages** for people who don't believe or understand what you're telling them. All the screen shots in this book were captured through the Print Screen key.

**processor**    Short for **microprocessor** or **central processing unit** (CPU).

**program**    **1.** What you use to apply your computer to do some useful task – hence **application**, the long word often used to mean 'program'. Also called software. Basically a collection of instructions written in a **programming language** that the machine understands and responds to, following your commands. *See also* **utility**.    **2.** To create software, using a programming language.

**Program Manager**  The main interface in the old Windows 3.1 and Windows for Workgroups, replaced in Windows 95 by the **desktop**, **taskbar** and **Start button**. Some Windows buffs still talk of it fondly.

**programmer**  Someone who writes **programs**, using **programming languages**. Creating software is a conceptual and design-focused activity as well as a technical one.

**programming language**  What human **programmers** use to speak to computers. There are various languages, all with their own grammar, syntax and vocabulary. Some resemble English, others hieroglyphics. Each **central processing unit** requires a specific language. Microsoft's Visual Basic graphical language, and C++, which can be used in both the PC and Macintosh environments, are prominent examples, as is Sun's **Java**, used for creating multi platform programs for Internet users.

**progress indicator**  Feedback by the computer about how a task is progressing, such as converting a large file to or from another format, or downloading information from a Website. This may be presented graphically, often in the form of a 'thermometer bar', or mathematically as an increasing percentage.

**prompt**  An indication from the computer that it is waiting for you to do something. The stern DOS prompt (C:\>) has been replaced in **GUI** environments by polite messages asking if, for example, you would like to continue.

**properties**    How an object in Windows has been set up to perform. Generally the properties for something can be accessed by **right-clicking** on it and choosing the Properties command. Properties for an open file can usually be found through the File menu.

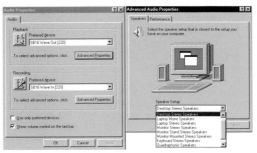

*Audio properties for a PC*

**protection**    In a network, where data is shared, you may need to prevent others from accessing a file, or making unauthorized changes to it. You can restrict access to a folder or file by protecting it with a **password**, or you can make a file **read-only** so that others can read but not edit it.

**protocol**    A common set of standards by which information is transferred between two points (say, two modems or two computers) on the Internet, or between two **local area networks** connected by a **router**. If both devices use the same protocol, the transfer proceeds quickly and smoothly. Examples are **Ethernet** and **TCP/IP**.

**Psion** Pioneers and innovators in the field of mobile communications, the name Psion has become identified with **hand-held computers**.

**public domain** Information or software that is not protected by copyright is in the public domain. You may use it freely and free of charge. Legally the term has no meaning in the UK, but there are no national boundaries on the Internet.

**publish** To copy a file to a **Web server** so that others may view it as a Web page or Website, by using a browser.

**pull-down menu** A longer term for menu, which literally describes what happens when you click on a menu: it drops down to offer you a choice of commands. *See also* **pop-up menu**.

# Q

**query** To extract specific information from a database is to query it. (The actual process is also called a query.) You might, say, want only surname and postcode **fields**. Or you can use 'criteria' to narrow the information: for example, all **records** dated between March 13 and May 24, plus only records that contain the words Bath and Bristol. The database then searches every record to find those that match your criteria.

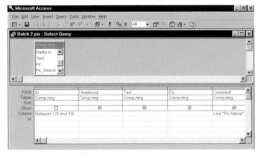

*This query specifically asks only for records numbered between 170 and 430 containing the words 'Pic name': all other records will automatically be excluded*

**queue** Several files waiting to be printed (in a **print queue**) or processed in some other way.

**Quick Launch toolbar**   A Windows 98 and 2000 feature that allocates an adjustable section of the **toolbar** for one-click icon shortcuts to your favourite programs and tools. Because the toolbar is always visible, these icons are always there for you, like friends and family.

*Your favourite programs and tools are always on-screen, thanks to the icons in Windows 98's Quick Launch toolbar*

**QuickTime**   Software built into the Mac operating system that will play movie clips stored in QuickTime format. Also available for the PC as an add-on.

**Quit**   The Mac way of saying 'Close this program'. The PC equivalent is **Exit**.

**QWERTY**   Historic typewriter-era term for the standard keyboard layout, referring to the first six letters in the top row. No one yet has come up with a better arrangement that everyone actually wants to use.

# R

**ragged right**   A visual way of saying that text is aligned on the left, so that its right margin looks ragged (as in this book). Sounds messy but is quite normal. *See* **alignment**.

**RAM**   Acronym for Random-Access Memory. Temporary, fast **memory** that handles your work since you last saved it and allows **random access** to any bit of it. It is volatile – everything is lost when the power is turned off. Saving your work moves it permanently from RAM to disk. The amount of RAM (measured in megabytes) on a computer is critical to its efficiency. Laser printers also use 'printer RAM' to store complex layouts and fonts in their **buffers**. *See also* **video RAM**.

**random access**   A way of reading at random what is in **memory**, regardless of where it is located. Analogous to finding track 10 on a music CD, which is instant, whereas on a cassette tape you have to fast-forward through the first nine tracks.

**read**   To move information from disk into **memory**. Used particularly of misbehaving floppy disks, as in, 'My computer can't read the files on this floppy.'

**Read Me file** A file, named 'README.TXT' or similar, that you're urged to read, to catch up with last-minute software additions, apologies and disclaimers, errors they meant to fix but couldn't finish in time…

**read-only** Describes a file you can open and read but not change. If you make a change and then try to save it, the computer will insist on your using a new filename, so that the original remains untouched. Also, it cannot be erased. In Mac terminology, the file is said to be 'locked'.

**reboot** To restart a PC in one of two ways. A cold boot – for a completely fresh start – involves switching it off, waiting some seconds while the hard disk stops spinning, then switching it on again. More sympathetic to the machine, a warm boot is done with the **reset switch**. The machine is reset, but the power supply is not interrupted. Macs do all this through keyboard commands.

**Recently Visited list** Colloquial term for a **History list** of previously visited sites on the Internet. Another (limited) place to look at is the box where you type Internet addresses: if you click on the black triangle on the right, a list of recently visited addresses will drop down.

**record** **1.** A full entry in a database, including all the **fields**. For example, in a database of grandchildren, each record might consist of the following fields: name,

parents, age, gender, birthday, likes and dislikes.
**2.** To use sound- or video-recording software on
your computer.

**recover**   One of several terms for restoring a deleted
file, usually involving the PC's **Recycle Bin**. Others are
**restore** and **undelete**. On the polite Mac, you 'retrieve' a
file from the Wastebasket (or **Trash**).

**Recycle Bin**   Lifted straight from the Mac, Windows'
Recycle Bin is where 'deleted' files end up. In reality
they are still on disk and can be **recovered**, at least until
the preset maximum size for the Recycle Bin has been
exceeded, at which point the oldest files start to be

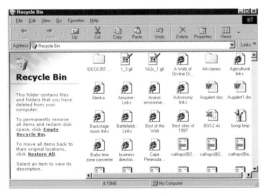

*Deleted files stay in the Recycle Bin until you empty it*

eliminated first. Emptying the whole Recycle Bin requires a specific command.

**redial** If a connection is busy, you can redial it either manually or by letting your modem do it automatically for a preset number of times.

**Redo** An **Office** command that allows you to restore a change you just reversed with the **Undo** command.

**reformat** **1.** To **format** a disk again, which will wipe clean all its contents. **2.** To alter the format (layout) of a document.

**Refresh, refresh rate** The Refresh button in most Web browsers reloads a Web page. Or, in **Windows Explorer** and **My Computer**, press the F5 button (or choose Refresh in the View menu) to display recent changes. 'Refresh rate' is the speed at which the monitor redraws its displays faster means better

**Registry** The Windows database where configuration information is stored about your computer and the devices it supports, the software you are running, and your own user details. It can be edited, but leave this to an expert.

**reload** To cause the information on a Website to be re-sent to your browser, usually by pressing the **Refresh** button.

**remote** A somewhat vague term roughly meaning 'not here – somewhere else'. A remote computer will be at least some distance away on a network, or connected to yours by **Dial-Up Networking**.

**removable disk**    Any disk that you can save data on and then physically remove from its drive.

**Reply, Reply All**    Buttons in an e-mail program, which you press to respond to an e-mail message. Reply automatically picks up the recipient's e-mail address. The Reply All button sends your response to anyone who received a copy of the original message.

**reset, reset switch**    To restart a computer (*see* **boot**). The reset switch on many PCs enables you to do a 'warm boot' (*see* **reboot**), or restart the machine without interrupting its power supply.

**resize box**    A small square at the bottom-right corner of a window in Mac OS. Click and drag on it to change the shape and size of the window. In Windows, click in the same place to get a double-ended arrow, then drag the corner.

*Drag on the resize box of any open window in the Mac OS*

**resolution**    Referring both to printers and monitors, indicating the clarity of the image they produce. Often shortened to 'res', as in 'high res/low res'. Measured in **dots per inch**: the more dots, the crisper the printed image or the screen display. Modern monitors are capable of a wide range of resolutions.

**resource**    A portmanteau word meaning anything that can be used: hardware items such as modems and monitors, capacity items such as memory and disk space (which are resources that need to be monitored, like fuel in a car), or network items such as shared printers or folders.

**restart** A software option in Windows that allows you to restart the computer. This method involves a warm boot (*see* **boot** *and* **reboot**).

**restore** **1.** To retrieve a file from a backup so that you can access it again. **2.** In Windows, to retrieve a deleted file from the **Recycle Bin**.

**Rich Text Format (RTF)** A partially successful attempt at a universal file format, RTF files save not only their data but also their essential formatting, such as font styles and sizes, colours, etc. Most word processors, and some other programs, can open and lay out RTF files accurately.

**right-click**
In Windows, to click the right mouse button rather than the normal left one, either because the program tells you to do so, or to display a shortcut menu. The menu will be context-

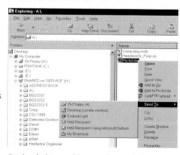

*Right-clicking a file on a floppy disk*

sensitive, meaning that it will be relevant to wherever you are on-screen and whatever you are doing within the program you are using. It is therefore well worth cultivating the habit of right-clicking.

**ROM**    Acronym for Read-Only Memory: memory that can be read by the computer but not written to. For example, a CD-ROM can only be read. Similarly, ROM chips in the computer contain permanent instructions needed when the computer starts up; they cannot be changed. *See also* **memory**.

**roman**    Normal (upright) type, just like this – the opposite of *italic* (slanted) type. Alternatively called 'regular' or 'plain'.

**root**    Computer file systems are hierarchical. Typically at the top is a **hard disk drive**. Down one level are **folders**, and below them, layers of **subfolders**, with **files** at the bottom of the pyramid. The 'root' is the term used for the top, and any files stored there (usually system files only) are said to be 'in the root'.

**router, routing**   A device connecting two networks that use the same **protocol**. Routers are used throughout the Internet to forward blocks or 'packets' of information from one host to another, a process known as routing. Each packet contains information about its destination, and the router works out the best available route at any given moment.

**RTF**   Acronym for **Rich Text Format**.

**run**   To start, **launch** or **load** a program. You also run, or play, a **macro**.

# S

**san-serif**   A font without **serifs**, such as Arial, Geneva or Verdana.

**save, Save As**   A saved file is stored permanently, usually on a hard disk, instead of only being held temporarily in volatile memory. For lasting peace of mind, save your work frequently (Ctrl+S – or Command+S on the Mac – is the smart and easy way). The Save As command enables you to save a file using a different name, location or format. You will see the Save As dialogue box the first time you save any new file.

**scan**   To use a **scanner** to read images or text into a computer. This requires special scanning software. There are two types: image-scanning software for scanning pictures, and **OCR** (Optical Character Recognition) software for scanning text and converting it into word processor format.

**ScanDisk** A crucial Windows utility that tracks down and repairs problems on

*Run ScanDisk regularly to keep your hard disk healthy*

floppy and hard disks. It can be set up to run regularly (say, weekly) on your hard disk, helping to maintain its good health.

**scanner** A device that reads printed images or text and passes the result to a computer, where it is converted by special software into digital format (*see* **scan**). You can then save it on disk for editing and using in your document. Once an expensive professional accessory, low-cost flat-bed scanners, which can scan entire pages, now often form part of complete computer packages.

**scan rate** The same as **refresh rate**: the speed with which a monitor redraws an image on-screen. Measured in hertz (Hz) – for example, 50 Hz is 50 times per second. The higher the scan rate, the better – and more expensive – the monitor.

*Flat-bed scanner*

**Scrapbook**
A Macintosh desk **accessory** in which you can store pictures or text that you want to use frequently.

*Frequently-used images and text can be stored in the Mac's Scrapbook.*

**screen buffer**
An area of memory reserved for storing the image displayed on-screen. Also called **video memory** (or video RAM).

**screen dump, screen shot**    What you get when you press the **Print Screen key**: a graphic image of exactly what's on the screen at the time. The term 'screen shot' is used more often and more politely than the alternative.

**screen font**    A font that represents on-screen as closely as possible what you get when you print. This was once a tiresome and confusing issue, but **TrueType** fixed the problem in one shot.

**screen saver**    The moving images that dance on the world's monitors when left untouched for more than a few minutes are supposedly there to prevent something called 'burn-in' – the formation of a permanent ghost image when the display stays unchanged for a long time. This is a problem that on newer monitors has largely ceased to exist. In reality, screen savers have become objects of enjoyment in their own right.

**scroll, scrolling, scroll bar, scroll box**   When there is more in a file than you can see on one screen, you scroll up or down to change the portion that's visible on-screen. Or when the image is wider than the screen can accommodate, scrolling horizontally will reveal the hidden portion. The scroll bar is the grey bar with an arrow at either end (used to move up or down in small jumps) and a slidable scroll box within it: click and drag on the scroll box to move at your own speed.

**SCSI**   Pronounced 'scuzzy', the acronym for Small Computer System Interface, a type of fast connector (or **port**) for devices like disk drives, scanners, tape drives and so on. These can be 'daisy-chained', meaning that up to six devices can plug one into the other. Standard on many Apple computers, and an alternative to **IDE** on PCs.

**SDRAM**   Stands for 'Synchronous DRAM'. **RAM** that is about twice as fast as **EDO RAM** and three times faster than **DRAM**.

**search, search string**   The word 'search' is generally synonymous with **find**, but most often refers to the act of looking for something on the World Wide Web. A search string is the term you type in for the **search engine** to look for. There may be particular rules ('syntax') to follow if you use multiple words: help should be readily to hand in the search engine.

**search and replace**    What older programs called **find and replace**.

**search engine**    A Website dedicated to hunting for information on the World Wide Web. You type in what you want to find; this is known as the **search string**. The search engine works fast to try to match your terms within a vast, continuously updated index of pages and their locations. When offered a list of links (a 'hit list'), click on the link of your choice to jump to the page. Leading search engines, all using different methods of matching terms, include *AltaVista, Excite, Goto, HotBot, Lycos, QuestFinder* and *Yahoo!*

*Search facilities vary and are not always clearly laid out. QuestFinder is one of the better presented search engines.*

**secure browser**   A Web browser that can send and receive private information such as credit card numbers securely, without intruders being able to decipher it. **Netscape Navigator** and **Internet Explorer** both qualify as secure. The prefix **https://** indicates a secure site.

**select, selected**   To mark a portion of text so that you can perform some action on it. Other verbs for 'select' are 'highlight' (because the text looks like this ), 'block' and 'swipe'. To select a graphic or frame, click on it to make **handles** appear. Other programs such as spreadsheets have their own selection methods.

**Select All**   The menu command that **selects** everything in a document, which is useful for wholesale deletion or copying. The Windows shortcut is Ctrl+A. On the Mac it's Command+A.

**self-extracting**   Describes a **compressed file** with a .EXE extension, meaning that it is **executable**. Normally the right compression software is needed to extract (or **unzip**) a compressed file, but a self-extracting one will do it by itself when the recipient double-clicks it.

**serial**   One by one. In computing, this refers to data that is transmitted one bit at a time, sometimes over long distances. *Compare with* **parallel**.

**serial port**   A port used for transmitting **serial** data, mostly used for a mouse or external modem. *See also* **parallel port**.

**serif**   The small embellishment at the end of certain letters, such as 'p' or 'I', whose practical function is to make them easier to read. Most typefaces (such as Garamond, the one used in this book) are serif. *Contrast with* **san-serif**.

**server**   A computer on a **network** that manages network **resources**. In a small **local area network**, a single dedicated computer may act as **file server**, print server (managing one or more printers) and network server (managing network traffic). In larger networks these may be separate machines. Servers on the Internet store and transmit particular types of information: for example, Web pages are stored on a **Web server**.

**setting**   **1.** How a program is configured – its appearance, behaviour and **default** assumptions – are

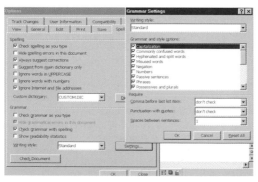

*Settings: you can set your preferences for automated spell- and grammar-checking in your word processor*

determined by its settings. Many of these can be changed by the user: look for Options, Preferences or Settings, usually in the Tools menu. Sometimes called **setup**.   **2.** Settings are also made within programs whenever you use a **dialogue box**.

**setup/set up**   **1.** To **install** software in Windows. **2.** To configure hardware to work with a computer. **3.** How a computer is configured.   **4.** Alternative for **settings**: 'What is your modem's setup?' means the same as 'What are your modem's settings?'

**SGML**   Acronym for Standard Generalized Markup Language, an open, international standard for organizing and tagging (marking up) the elements of a document.

**shareware**   Software distributed on the honour system through the Internet, or from CD-ROMs on magazine or book covers. If you find the program useful, you are supposed to register it and pay the author a small fee.

**sheet feeder**   A special paper tray for a printer, which lets you use, say, letterhead fed one at a time into the printer instead of standard printer paper.

**shell**   The graphical 'front end' of an operating system or program that acts as an **interface** between it and you. Still commonplace in **command-driven** environments such as Unix or DOS, but more or less redundant in the **GUI** world, because GUIs themselves are shells.

**Shift key**   A **modifier key** you press in combination with other keys to give commands to the computer. Its most important job is to produce capital letters when combined with alphabetic keys. 'Shift' is another of those good old typewriter-era words.

**ShockWave**　A **plug-in** for a Web browser, with which you can view sophisticated animations.

*ShockWave looks exciting – and delivers*

**shortcut**　A shortcut allows a document or program to be shared from different locations, using different names if wanted. The original survives unchanged whenever you delete a shortcut. (Called an **alias** in Mac OS.)

**shortcut keys**　Combinations of keys that include **modifier keys**, which execute commands quicker than the conventional mouse and menu method. Four of the most valuable are Ctrl+X (cut), Ctrl+C (copy), Ctrl+V (paste) and Ctrl+S (save). On the Mac, substitute Command for Ctrl. Keyboard shortcuts are displayed in the menus.

**shortcut menu**   A menu relevant to your current context (sometimes called a context menu), reached by a **right-click** on the mouse. Most often used after selecting something on-screen.

**shrink-wrapped**   Refers to the clear plastic covering around new software boxes. Because you are purchasing a licence to use the software, tearing the wrapping off marks the actual moment you take ownership.

**shut down**   The command to exit Windows and, on most newer PCs, turn off the computer automatically.

**signature**   A small file containing information to be added automatically to the end of your outgoing e-mail messages. Typically this will contain your name, work title and contact details.

**sign on**   To call a server on a network or the Internet and type in your **user name** and **password**. Once you have successfully signed on, you can use the services.

**SIMM**   Acronym for Single Inline Memory Module, a kind of memory chip (or **RAM**). Superseded by DIMMs but still used on older systems. You must get the right kind of SIMM, as they come in different formats.

**slot**   A long, thin hole at the back of a computer, covered with a removable plate, which conceals an **expansion slot** or socket on the **motherboard** into which you plug an **adaptor**. The more slots the better, as this determines how many devices you can connect to the computer.

**small caps**   A form of **typeface** in which letters are set in SMALLER-SIZED CAPITAL LETTERS. If they look LIKE THIS, they are set in initial caps and small caps, whereas LIKE THIS they are set in all caps.

**smiley**   :-) is the best-known **emoticon**.

**SMTP**   Acronym for Simple Mail Transfer Protocol, the **protocol** for sending e-mail messages between servers. Outgoing messages are sent to your **ISP**'s SMTP server. You need to specify both this and the ISP's **POP3** server when configuring your e-mail software.

*Specifying your ISP's SMTP server*

**soft copy**   Something in digital form (on disk) and therefore volatile, unlike **hard copy** (on paper), which is permanent.

**soft return**   In word processing, like typewriting, the word 'return' refers to moving to the start of the next line. Word processors do it automatically, inserting 'soft returns', until you press the Enter key at the end of the paragraph, when a **hard return** is entered. Subsequent changes to the length of a paragraph

will move the soft returns as required, but the hard
return will stay put.

**software**   *See* **application** *and* **program**. The
word 'soft' refers to the intangibility of a computer
program – unlike computer hardware, you cannot
touch software.

**sort**   To put information into an order, usually
alphabetical or numerical. Word-processed lists or
tables, records in a database, or columns of entries in a
spreadsheet can all be sorted in either descending (A–Z)
or ascending (Z–A) order.

**SoundBlaster**   Creative Labs' SoundBlaster set the
standard for **sound cards** on the PC, and most rival
cards are compatible with it. SoundBlaster supports the
musical-instrument **MIDI** standard.

*Creative Labs' SoundBlaster set the standard for sound cards on
the PC*

**sound card**    An **expansion card** that adds music and sound to your computer's capabilities. Goes hand-in-hand with a **CD-ROM** and is universal on new computers.

**source**    The location from which you take data when you copy or move it. The location you send it to is the **destination** (or **target**).

**space character, spacebar**    The space between words, entered by pressing the spacebar, is treated as an actual character by the computer, although all you perceive is a space.

**spam**    Unsolicited e-mail – the electronic equivalent of junk mail. Spamming is seriously frowned upon.

**special character**    Any unusual character that cannot be typed straight from the keyboard, such as the copyright symbol ©, the Greek character π, or an arrow character like ».

**spell-check, spell checker**    A feature in word processors and other programs, which compares your text with an extensive dictionary, highlights errors or words it doesn't recognize, and suggests alternatives – occasionally with comical results. You can teach the dictionary new words.

**spike**    A sudden burst of electrical power, most probably caused by a nearby lightning strike. The effect can vary from a flicker on the screen to computer Armageddon. A low-cost surge suppressor (or 'spike protector') will help – but the safest protection in a violent electrical storm is to unplug your equipment.

Ian Botham
Ryan Giggs
Leonardo DiCa
Hillary Clinton
Tyrannosaurus
Boyzone
Alan Shearer
Nelson Mandel
Ghostbusters

Spelling and Grammar: English (British)

Not in Dictionary;
Ian Bottom

Suggestions:
Bottom
Both
Bother
Bothell
Bothers
Bathmat

☑ Check grammar    Options...

Ignore
Ignore All
Add
Change
Change All
AutoCorrect
Undo
Cancel

*Perils of spell-checking: Ian Bottom?*

**spreadsheet**   A program presented as a grid of rows
and columns that intersect to form **cells**. You can enter
any kind of information into each cell, changing its size
and characteristics as required. Formulae for
sophisticated calculations of any number of cells can be
entered, which recalculate automatically when a value in
any one cell is changed. The leading spreadsheets are
Microsoft's **Excel**, **Lotus** *1-2-3* and Corel's *Quattro Pro*.
*See also* **worksheet**.

**Start button, Start menu**   The button labelled
Start in the corner of the Windows screen, from which
you can start programs, jump straight to recently used
files or **Favorites**, and access Windows' main features.
The Start button leads to the Start menu.

**startup disk**   **1.** The disk on which the computer
expects to find the operating system – usually the main
hard disk.   **2.** PCs look first for a floppy disk, then
automatically move on to the hard disk. In Windows,

*Access all your programs through the Start menu*

you can create an emergency startup disk on a floppy disk, with only the essential elements of the operating system. Also called a boot disk, this will get a PC running, even with a failing hard disk.

**status bar**   The strip at the foot of open program windows, which displays information about the file such as which page you are on and the total number of pages. The status bar in some programs, such as *WordPerfect*, can be configured to display information of your choice, including buttons for formatting text.

**storage**   The **media** you keep data on: hard disk(s), removable disks, tapes, etc. Disk drives are sometimes called 'storage devices'.

**style, style sheet**   A collection of **formatting** choices
applied to a section of word-processed text – say,
headings and subheadings – can be saved and stored as
a style and then applied again in future. A style sheet, in
a word processor or desktop publishing program,
extends this principle to whole documents, automating
the process of laying out complex publications.

**stylus**   A **pointing device** most accurately described as
a stylus but more often called a **pen**.

**subdirectory, subfolder**   A **folder** within a folder (or
in older Windows-speak, a **directory** below a directory).

**submenu**   Click on the right-pointing triangle (▶) to
the right of some menu commands to display a
submenu of further commands. Sometimes further
submenus lead off a submenu.

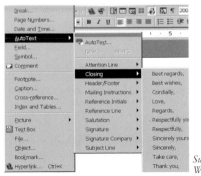

*Submenus in Word*

**subscribe**    To read information in a **newsgroup**, you must first download the list of newsgroups available from a news server and choose those to which you want to subscribe. Unlike real newspaper subscriptions, this is a software rather than commercial action – you don't pay. You can then receive and read the newsgroup's messages.

**subscript**    Smaller text that appears slightly below neighbouring text – for example, in chemical formulae such as $CO_2$. *Compare with* **superscript**.

**suite**    Short for 'office suite', and technically known as **integrated software**.

**superscript**    Smaller text that appears slightly above neighbouring text, as, for example, in $10^2$. *Compare with* **subscript**.

**Super VGA**    A monitor/adapter combination that will support a high-resolution display (*see* **resolution** *and* **VGA**).

**support**    **1.** Technical help for your machine or program, via telephone, the Internet, or actual humans who will fix something that doesn't work properly. It should be part of the package you buy, though generally only for a limited period of time – after that you'll have to pay extra. The level and type of support offered should be an important factor when deciding what and where to buy. **2.** To work with something else, as in 'FireWire is supported by Windows 98 and Mac OS 8.5'.

**surf, surfer**   To move from page to page on the World Wide Web, using a Web browser. A surfer can focus on tracking down some particular bit of information, or can just skim around randomly for recreational purposes.

**surge, surge suppressor**   A surge is the same as a **spike**, and a surge suppressor protects your computer against it.

**SVGA**   Short for **Super VGA**.

**swap file**   A section of the hard disk permanently reserved to provide extra memory. *See* **virtual memory**.

**swipe**   To **select** a section of text by clicking and holding the left button on the mouse, dragging the mouse cursor to the right and, if necessary, down, and finally releasing the mouse button. The word 'swipe' accurately conveys this physical action.

**syntax, syntax error**   Like its human counterpart, computer language is based on rules, which are called syntax. Every **programming language** has its own distinct set of rules. When these rules are not strictly followed, the computer will tell you that you have committed a 'syntax error' (or similar), meaning that it cannot understand what you have asked it to do.

**System 7/8/9**   System 7 laid the foundation for
Apple's current operating system, and can still be found
running plenty of older Macs. From version 8 onwards
the 'System' prefix was replaced by **Mac OS**. The
current Power Macintosh generation of computers runs
Mac OS 9, which has advanced Internet, networking
and colour-management features.

**system clock**   An internal clock, which runs only
when the computer is turned on. Its main task is to
record the time when files are saved to disk. It takes its
time from the hardware clock, which runs continuously
on battery power when the system is turned off.

**system disk**   Another term for **boot disk** or **startup
disk**, namely the disk (usually the hard disk) that
contains the programs needed to start the computer and
its operating system.

**System Folder**   The Mac's special folder for system
files. Whenever the computer starts up, this is where it
looks for the operating system, the **Finder**, printer fonts,
and other basics. Here too live inbuilt desk accessories
such as the **Scrapbook**. The Windows folder on a PC
has roughly the same role.

**system font**   A built-in typeface, usually Arial,
without which the operating system cannot
communicate with you through menus, dialogue boxes
and so on. You may want to change it.

**system freeze**   The computer equivalent of paralysis,
namely when everything on the screen, including the
mouse cursor, stops working. Often interchanged with

**crash**, though strictly a crash is when a computer actually informs you that it has stopped working. If a Mac OS 8/8.5/9 system freeze is caused by a locked program, free the system by pressing Command+ Alt+Escape. If that doesn't work, restart the Mac by pressing Ctrl, Command and the Restart key (◄) all together.

**system tray** In Windows, the area to the far right of the **taskbar**, which contains icons for small programs that run within or alongside Windows. The two standard icons are for system date/time and speaker volume control. Other icons tend to be added willy-nilly when programs are installed; some are useful, others are incidental.

*System tray*

# T

**tab, Tab key    1.** In a word processor, a tab is a pre-set location for text **alignment**, reached by pressing the Tab key one or more times. It can be used for simple **tabulation** (from which the word derives), as on a typewriter.    **2.** In some **dialogue boxes**, card-index-like tabs, which you click on with the mouse, lead to different features.    **3.** In spreadsheets, a similar tab device at the foot of each **worksheet** allows you to switch between two or more worksheets. **4.** In tables, spreadsheets, databases and online registration forms, you can navigate with the Tab key from one **cell** or **field** to the next.

**table, tabulation**    Information organized into **cells** and divided by gridlines that may or may not be visible. Tables can be inserted into word processor documents and other programs, and are extensively used in Web pages. Tabulation is the process of organizing information in tabular form, which at its simplest can be achieved with the **Tab key**.

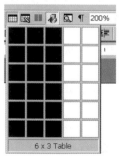

*Using the Table button on the* Word *toolbar*

**tape backup**   A low-cost way to backup, or archive for long-term storage, very large volumes of data, which can be set to run automatically, perhaps overnight. A tape drive added to the computer uses magnetic tapes that are superficially similar to audio tapes; different sizes are available. Restoring data from tape is comparatively slow.

**target**   The location to which you transfer data when you copy or move it. Also called **destination**. The location you take the data from is the **source**.

**task, task-switching**   Each activity you make a computer do is a separate task. The real virtue of modern computers is their ability to **multitask** – to do several things at the same time. You can switch, or move, between different tasks, using a variety of methods. For example, in Windows you can click on the icon for an open program on the **taskbar** to bring it into the **foreground**, or use the Alt+Tab key combination to **toggle** between programs.

**taskbar**   The icon-filled strip at one edge of the screen, usually the bottom. It contains the **Start button**,

**The Windows 98 taskbar**

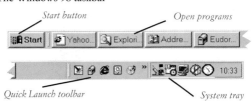

*Start button*          *Open programs*

*Quick Launch toolbar*          *System tray*

**thesaurus** A computer's version of a traditional thesaurus, or collection of synonyms. You highlight the word for which you seek a similar word, and the thesaurus attempts to come up with suggestions. Can work a treat, depending on what you ask it.

*A computer's thesaurus can sort out the user's word-blindness*

**thread** In online **newsgroup** discussions, an evolving series of responses to an original subject. New responses are added to the whole intact thread. A similar scenario may occur in exchanges of e-mails between several collaborating correspondents.

**TIFF** Acronym for Tagged Image File Format, a commonly used graphic file format for storing **bitmap graphics** for use on PCs and Macs. They can be of any **resolution**, in colour, **greyscale** or black and white.

**tile, tiling** To tile is to organize multiple windows like a set of tiles, so that they all share the available space on-screen without overlapping. Tiling might be useful for comparing information or copying data from one window to another, although the windows become awkwardly small.

**title bar**   The shaded bar at the top of every window that tells you what program you are in and the name of the open file (or 'Untitled', or something similar, if it's a new file), so that you know where you are. Dialogue boxes also have title bars. You can click and drag on a title bar to move the window around on-screen.

**toggle**   **1.** To alternate between two states, as in a **check box**, where an option is either checked (ticked) or not checked. On/off keys such as Caps Lock or Num Lock are also toggled.   **2.** In **multitasking**, to move or switch from one open program to another.

**toner, toner cartridge**   Black, powdery, electronically charged particles of ink used by laser printers and photocopiers. Avoid spillages (messy) and putting empty cartridges out with the household rubbish (they're toxic). Try to buy from an outlet (sadly, increasingly rare) that will take back the refillable cartridges for recycling, or find a charity that takes them.

**tool**   A button in a **toolbox**. Each one does a particular job. For example, in a drawing toolbox, you use the oval tool for drawing ovals; then you click on the 'fill colour' tool to fill the oval with, say, yellow.

**toolbar, toolbox**   The strip of buttons, usually along the top of an open program window, which provides one-click access to various commands and functions. Additional toolbars for particular tasks may be found in the View menu and can sometimes be dragged to another location on-screen, or be turned into a **floating toolbar**. A toolbox resembles a toolbar but contains specialized tools, for example for drawing.

Word's *Standard and Formatting toolbars (top and centre rows) and Drawing toolbox (bottom row)*

**touchpad**   A touch-sensitive pad connected to a mouse port. Your own finger provides the **pointing device**: you move it around on the pad to make the mouse cursor respond on-screen. Buttons correspond to normal mouse buttons. Portable computers usually have touchpads, though many users prefer to plug in a mouse.

**tower computer**   A computer with a tall, upright case. The generous amount of room 'under the bonnet' for adding extra hard drives, etc. makes full towers an ideal shape and size for use as network servers. *Compare with* **minitower computer**.

**trackball**   A **pointing device** with a large ball, which you rotate to move the mouse cursor (so there's no need for an intrusive cable and mouse pad). Often found on notebook computers. Many users find them the best alternative to a mouse.

**trash, Trash** To delete, or trash, a folder or file on a Mac, you click on it, then drag and drop it onto the Trash icon. Like a real trash can, stuff stays in Trash until you deliberately empty it, so second thoughts are possible. Long-windedly renamed Wastebasket for the UK market, although the latest machines have reverted to the US word 'Trash'.

**tree structure** The concept of the tree structure, which underlies the **folder tree**, existed long before GUIs became the predominant computer interface. Even **command-driven** operating systems store and display their directories and files in a hierarchical structure resembling a multi branched tree.

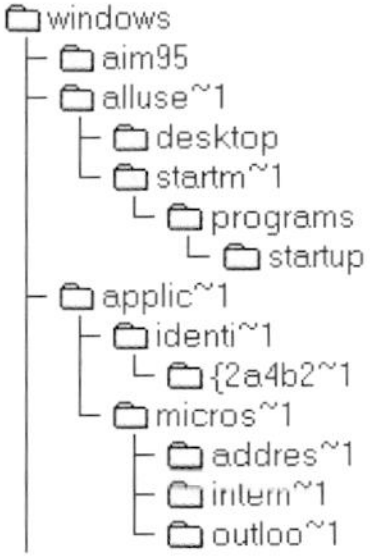
windows
aim95
alluse~1
desktop
startm~1
programs
startup
applic~1
identi~1
{2a4b2~1
micros~1
addres~1
intern~1
outloo~1

*Windows 3.1 very clearly showed the branches in its tree structure*

**TrueType** A font system jointly developed by Microsoft and Apple, TrueType revolutionized computer font-handling by building everything into the font file itself. Both screen and printer use the same TrueType fonts, eliminating mismatched on-screen approximations and the need for separate font installations. And TrueType fonts are 'scalable', growing or shrinking as required. Previously, separate fonts had to be installed for each size.

**tutorial**   A step-by-step teach-yourself package, in book or computer form, for learning new software. Some programs have mini-tutorials that teach specific complex processes. Mac OS Help makes extensive use of this approach, which it calls 'Interactive Help', and Windows Help is moving in the same direction.

**typeface**   Traditionally a typeface was a complete set of characters in a particular font, in all styles (roman, bold and italic), and in all sizes: contrast this with the traditional meaning of **font**. Although computers now use the word 'font' to mean the same as typeface, the distinction is worth retaining.

# U

**undelete**    To reverse a deletion you have just made. Matter deleted in a program can be restored by using the **Undo** command. Deleted files can be restored to their previous location provided they are still in the Windows Recycle Bin or Mac Trash/Wastebasket. Called 'unerase' in some programs.

**underline**    To underscore text, like this. Used for occasional display headings and in numerical work, but now only rarely for emphasis.

**underscore**    **1.** The character above the hyphen on the UK keyboard, used with Shift to create a continuous line, like this _____. Sometimes seen used singly as a separator in filenames and Web (and occasionally e-mail) addresses.    **2.** Another word for **underline**.

**Undo**    The command that reverses what you just did. Modern programs can go back several steps, though this needs to be handled with care. Some programs even have a **Redo** command that lets you undo an Undo. (Then you can redo the Undo…)

*Typical Undo (left) and Redo (right) buttons*

**undocumented**    Refers with intentional irony to anything in a program that isn't mentioned in the printed documentation, the Help system or the

*An undocumented option in Windows: you can add My Computer to the taskbar*

supporting Website. Operating systems and mainstream programs have become so complex that many useful features end up undocumented. Computer magazines and other users pass these on as hot tips.

**Unicode**    Intended as a replacement for the longstanding **ASCII** character standard for sharing data between all types of computer, Unicode can represent more than 65,000 characters. This enables it to handle every language, including Japanese, Chinese – and Klingon, for the trekkies out there.

**Uniform Resource Locator**    An Internet address, invariably referred to as **URL**.

**uninstall**    To enable the operating system to work properly with them, most programs put down roots all over Windows. Consequently, if you need to get rid of a program, the old-fashioned method of deleting its program folder will only do part of the job. Programs that uninstall properly through Add/Remove Programs (in the **Control Panel**) can be thoroughly eliminated from the system.

*Windows' Add/Remove Programs*

**universal serial bus** *See* **USB**.

**Unix** A long-lived **command-driven** operating system, capable of **multitasking** and supporting multiple platforms, from mainframes to personal computers. Portable, flexible and reliable, it is popular in universities and scientific institutions and provided the foundations for the entire Internet. Unix made few inroads into the personal computer market because of its large size and cryptic interface, but recent **GUIs** for Unix and the fast-emerging **Linux** version are enabling it to challenge Windows.

**unjustified** The same thing as **ragged right**. *See also* **alignment**.

**unsubscribe** The opposite of **subscribe**. You must unsubscribe to prevent unwanted messages downloading to you from a newsgroup.

**unzip** To decompress a **compressed file**. The word is used generally, but strictly refers to one of the Zip family of compression programs such as PKZIP or WinZip.

**upgrade** To improve, by adding something newer, better and usually bigger, though not always faster. You upgrade software by installing a newer version, and hardware by replacing or adding new components – or you can upgrade your entire system by replacing everything.

**upload** To transfer a file from your computer to another computer on the Internet. For example, you upload a new Web page to a Web server. The opposite of **download**.

**uppercase** CAPITAL LETTERS – THE OPPOSITE OF **lowercase**.

**uptime** All the time a computer is working is uptime – the opposite of **downtime**.

**URL** Acronym for Uniform Resource Locator (pronounced U–R–L or 'earl'), the proper term for an **Internet address**. Each URL basically has three parts: the **protocol**, or type of site; the **domain name**, which usually denotes which country the site is in and what sort of organization it represents; and the **pathname** or location of the web page you seek. These three parts are explained in more detail in the table opposite.

**Below is a breakdown of the following URL:**

```
http://www.soapbox.co.uk/david/biznews/
new_soap.htm
```

### PART 1 – PROTOCOL

`http://` = a hypertext file on the World Wide Web

ALTERNATIVES:  `https://` = a secure WWW file
  `ftp://` = an FTP site
  Usenet omits the part up to //

*In current Web browsers you don't have to type `http://` as this is the default. Type uppercase and lowercase accurately – it may be critical*

### PART 2 – DOMAIN

`www.soapbox.co.uk/` = the domain, or site name, of the Soapbox Company in the UK

Other country codes include: ie (Ireland), de (Germany), fr (France), au (Australia) etc.

A site name ending with:

`.ac` = academic institution
`.co` = commercial organization
`.com` = company (usually US-based or global)
`.edu` = educational institution
`.gov` = government agency

### PART 3 – PATHNAME:

`david/biznews/new_soap.htm` = an HTML Web page located in the david/biznews subfolder

ALTERNATIVE EXTENSIONS:  `.txt` = a plain text file
  `.exe` = an executable file

*A pathname may be short or long and may contain numbers, symbols and punctuation*

**USB** Acronym for Universal Serial Bus. A relatively new type of **serial** connection, which allows up to 127 devices to be 'daisy-chained' (one plugged into the other) and which supports pretty well every kind of external device. It fully supports **Plug and Play** and 'hot plugging' (allowing you to plug and unplug devices as you wish without having to restart the computer). Likely to replace **parallel ports** and **serial ports**.

**Usenet** Contraction of USEr NETwork, a worldwide network of servers that manage information exchanges between **newsgroups**. Articles ('postings') are sent to Usenet as contributions to public discussions and are grouped by topic into more than 25,000 newsgroups. Usenet is a **bulletin board** system and can be accessed through many **ISPs**.

**user** Any user of a computer, whether novice or expert.

**user-friendly, user-hostile** 'User-friendly' refers to any equipment or program that you can explore intuitively, is easy to use and is pleasing to the eye. If it's cryptic, clumsy and ugly, it's user-hostile. **GUIs** are reputedly the former and command-driven environments the latter, but like everything else in computing, that is a matter of opinion.

**user group** A group of users of a particular type of hardware or software, who exchange information and meet regularly for discussions.

**user ID** Another term for **user name**.

**user interface**   What you see when you sit in front of a computer monitor. Each operating system offers a different style of user interface: in particular, a **GUI** OS looks radically different to a **command-driven** OS. Programs also show variations in their user interface, deploying differing tools and commands, and creating their own proprietary special features.

**user name, username**   The name you use to log to a network, **bulletin board**, **newsgroup** or other online service. Unlike a **password**, your user name is public.

*Logging on to a network*

**user profile**   Information about yourself that you provide for other users when joining a **chat room**, **bulletin board** or other online service. You might choose to omit specifics that too readily identify you and instead use an alias and a separate, anonymous e-mail address.

**utility**   A program that helps to maintain the computer, or performs and streamlines a specific task. Examples include **antivirus** and **compression** programs, font-management programs such as *Adobe Type Manager*, file-transfer programs such as *LapLink*, and disk-maintenance programs like *Norton Utilities* or the ScanDisk utility in Windows.

Adobe Type Manager, *the font utility for PostScript*

# V

**V.90**   A standard for the current generation of
56 Kbps modems, which resolved two previously
competing standards. Look for V.90 compliance if you
are purchasing a modem.

**vector graphic**   Created in a **draw program**, a
graphic drawn by using lines. Each drawn line is a
separate object, which can be formatted, moved or
resized. These characteristics make vector graphics
easier to edit and smaller in file size than **bitmap
graphics**.

**version**   An edition of a software product. Versions
used always to be expressed in numbers, a full number
like 4.0 indicating a major new edition, while a decimal
increase like 4.1 indicated an interim update. Lately,
calendar years have been more often used to denote
different versions, as in Office 97 and Office 2000.

**VGA**   Acronym for Video Graphics Array, the basic
standard for displaying colour. Long superseded by
**Super VGA**, it survives as a basic setting option for
monitor displays, which is occasionally needed for
specialized tasks.

**video conferencing**   A form of **conferencing**
involving two or more people at different sites using
computers to transmit both sound and vision. Each
participant has a camera, microphone and speakers
connected to a computer. The speakers' faces, or

examples they want to display, appear on-screen while others hear them talk, and they can also use the normal interactive program-sharing found in conventional conferencing. Can be used over internal networks or long-distance via telephone lines.

**video memory, video RAM**   A special part of the computer's **RAM**, in which images displayed on-screen are stored.

**virtual memory**   Space reserved on the hard disk, called a **swap file**, which is used to expand a PC's **RAM** capabilities. The basic idea is to free up true RAM for programs that need it. Computers with insufficient RAM slow down noticeably because they need to use the swap file heavily, which involves much copying back and forth of information.

**virtual reality**   A simulated three-dimensional world, entered by putting on headware and gloves connected to a computer, with which your responses and movements interact. Used in advanced gaming software and for engineering simulations. The term may also be used less accurately of any visuals that look 3-D on a conventional screen.

**virus**   An unwanted, destructive program put onto a computer by a clever time-waster with programming skills. Many viruses can replicate themselves, spreading through e-mail and address books and causing damage, sometimes severe, to computer systems and networks. Keep your **antivirus** program up to date, follow all its instructions, and always backup zealously.

**voice recognition**   Software that allows you to dictate to your computer. It recognizes human speech and translates it into digital signals that the computer understands. The technology, although still having distinct limitations, is developing rapidly as a mainstream alternative to using keyboards.

**volume control**   The software control for your loudspeakers. This can offer sophisticated controls, depending on your audio equipment.

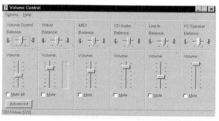

*Volume controls for your speakers*

**VRAM**   Acronym for Video Random-Access Memory. *See* **video RAM**.

**VRML**   Acronym for Virtual Reality Modelling Language (pronounced 'vermal' or V–R–M–L), a three-dimensional form of **HTML**, which allows 3-D images to be displayed on the World Wide Web. With a VRML browser, or a VRML **plug-in** to a standard browser, you can display a 3-D 'world' on your screen and move around within it, using the arrow keys.

# W

**wallpaper**   Decoration for the **desktop** is called 'wallpaper' in Windows and plain old 'pictures and patterns' in Mac OS. You can choose from a wide range of graphic images, or download a whole lot more from the Web.

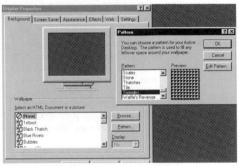

*Choose your own wallpaper*

**WAN**   Acronym for Wide Area Network, a network that spans more than one location – say, a company's offices in Edinburgh and Glasgow. *See also* **network**.

**Wastebasket**   Apple's Brit-sensitive renaming of their traditional **Trash**. They must think we like long words.

**watch icon**   The Mac equivalent of the Windows **hourglass icon**, meaning, 'Hold on, I'm busy.'

**Web**   The colloquial contraction for **World Wide Web**.

**Web authoring**   Creating personal or corporate Websites. Examples of Web authoring software include Microsoft's *FrontPage*, now part of **Office**, and Macromedia's *Dreamweaver*, both rich with features for creating text, graphics and other Net content. Content-heavy documents can also be published directly to the Web with **desktop publishing** programs.

**Web browser**   Software designed to view documents written in **HTML** stored on Websites on the Internet. Browsers load each Web page, more or less accurately displaying graphics, text formatting, animations and sound clips. **Hyperlinks** allow you to jump to other pages. Browsers also display other types of Internet content, including **FTP** and **newsgroup** information. The two leading browsers are **Netscape Navigator** and **Internet Explorer**.

**Webcast**   To broadcast information on the Internet, using sound and video. Often this will form part of a live event, for example a major charity concert. Sometimes you can participate by using **chat** facilities to send questions to celebrities.

**Webcrawler**   A program for automatically searching the World Wide Web, which feeds pages to a **search engine**. Sometimes called a spider: both terms reflect its role of crawling all over the Web, looking for links relevant to the word or words for which you are searching. AOL's WebCrawler does just this, and other search engines have their equivalents.

**Web page**   A single document on the World Wide Web, regardless of its length (the term has nothing to do with conventional pagination). Every Web page is identified by a unique **URL**.

**Web server**   A computer connected to the Internet, which sends **Web pages** to other computers when requested. When you type the (fictitious) **URL** `http://www.soapbox.co.uk/index.html` into your browser, it sends a request to the Web server whose **domain name** is `www.soapbox.co.uk`. The server finds the page 'index.html' and passes it to your browser.

**Website**   A collection of **Web pages** on the World Wide Web, owned by an individual or organization. There may be one or many pages. The first one users will see, unless they request a specific page, is the **home page**.

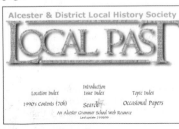

*Example of a home page*

**Web space**   Disk space for storing **Web pages**, provided by an **Internet service provider**, often free of charge as part of the service for which you pay. An **HTML** document stored in your Web space will then be available to anyone who knows the **URL**.

**WebTV, Web TV**   A general term (spelled in two ways) for the whole field of connecting your TV set to the Internet.

**wide area network**   The full term for a **WAN**. The short form is normally used.

**wildcard**   A character used to represent unknown characters when searching for files or on the Web. A question mark (?) represents a single unknown character, as in soap???.txt, which would find soap005.txt, soap125.txt and soapbox.txt. An asterisk (*) represents multiple characters, as in *.* (pronounced star dot star), which would find all the files in a folder or on a disk.

**Win**   A prefix for anything to do with **Windows**.

**window**   A rectangular area on-screen, which displays a program, or information in a file. Windows can be individually sized, moved around and positioned, or be converted into **icons** and restored to full size when required. You can switch between windows, and copy/cut and paste information or files between windows.

**Windows**   Microsoft's popular operating system, once a rather crude imitation of Apple's influential Mac OS but now its close match. The earlier versions 3.1 and

*Program (or application) window*

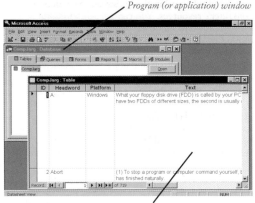

*File window – here, a table opened in a database*

3.11 for Workgroups, still in widespread use on older machines, were essentially GUIs for DOS, as, arguably, was the much more advanced Windows 95. The current Windows 98 and forthcoming Windows 2000 are true 32-bit operating systems, with Internet and advanced hardware-support features. The powerful Windows NT Server and NT Workstation are Microsoft's networking contenders. Windows CE is a simplified, compact version for hand-held computers.

**Windows Explorer** Windows' distinctive folder and file manager capitalizes on its DOS heritage. It displays a graphical **tree structure**, which illustrates the integrated relationship that exists between all of a computer's **resources**. You can access everything through this one window: your disk drives and everything on them, all your programs, the whole of a network if you are connected to one, the Internet, all your data, and controls and utilities for configuring and maintaining your computer.

**Windows keys** Both Windows keys (with the Windows logo) pop up the **Start menu**. (On older keyboards, Ctrl+Esc does the same thing.) A third special key, showing a menu and cursor arrow, to the right of the right-hand Windows key, pops up a **submenu** for whatever is highlighted on-screen (the same as if you **right-click** with the mouse).

**wizard** In Windows, a wizard helps you to do something easily, taking most of the task over from you and leaving you to make a series of simple choices. Wizards are available in many utilities and applications, and

*Word's Letter Wizard*

also appear automatically in some hardware
configuration routines.

**Word**    The standard-setting market-leader in **word
processors** and an integral part of the **Office** suite. Full
of powerful and sophisticated features – some might say,
too full.

**word processor**    A program for writing, editing,
organizing and laying out documents – the most
common application for computers. The three major
contenders are Microsoft's *Word*, Corel's *WordPerfect*
and Lotus *WordPro* (formerly *AmiPro*). Compared with
simple **text editors**, full-scale word processors have
many powerful features including the ability to handle
graphics, check spellings, create tables of contents and
indexes, and much else.

**word wrap**    In word processors, text editors and
desktop publishing programs, word wrap causes text to
fit automatically within the margins of the page. When a
line is filled with text, the next word automatically
jumps to the next line.

**worksheet**    The term used by *Excel* and *Lotus 1-2-3*
for an individual **spreadsheet** in a file. In *Quattro Pro*,
it's just a 'sheet'. You can have numerous worksheets in
a single file, all reached via **tabs** near the foot of the
screen.

**workstation**    **1.** A powerful computer with excellent
graphics capabilities, used for scientific or engineering
programs such as **CAD** or software development.
Workstations are usually grouped into networks but can

be used as stand-alone systems.   **2.** In networking, any computer connected to a **local area network**.

**World Wide Web (WWW)**   The visible, content-rich face of the Internet, usually abbreviated to 'the Web' or WWW. It is a network of **Web servers**, which store linked documents written in **HTML** (**Web pages**) that can be accessed via **Web browsers**. Websites and documents are comprehensively indexed and can be searched by **keyword**. Collections of preselected Websites grouped into topics are called **directories**.

**write error**   What happens when you try to save onto a disk that is full, damaged or **write-protected**.

**write-protect**   **1.** To prevent others from overwriting a file, by making it **read-only**.   **2.** To protect a floppy disk or other storage medium from being accidentally overwritten.

**WWW**   The familiar written acronym for the **World Wide Web**.

**WYSIWYG**   Pronounced 'wizzywig', the acronym for 'What You See Is What You Get'. In a modern **GUI**, what you see on the screen is (almost) exactly what you'll get on the printed page. Not long ago, this represented Mecca; now it's taken for granted.

# X

**XML** Acronym for eXtensible Markup Language, a new code for Web documents that will probably supplant **HTML**. For Web designers and users, its advantages include the ability to insert codes that link to multiple documents (an HTML code will link to just one). This will greatly enhance the process of searching. XML-coded documents can also be published in terrestrial media such as print and CD-ROM.

# Z

**zip** 'Zipping' is an apt term for **compression**, or reducing the amount of disk storage space or transmission time required for a file. Although now used generally, it derives from the Zip family of compression utilities (PKZIP, PKUNZIP and WinZip). WinZip is the leader on PCs. Its counterpart on Macs is Stuffit.

*WinZip makes it easy to handle compressed files*

**Zip disk, Zip drive** A **removable disk** manufactured by Iomega, with a capacity of about 100 **megabytes**, making it far more useful than a floppy disk for

transporting and archiving data. Zip drives can be either
internal or external.

**zoom, zoom box**    To zoom is to change a
document's size on the screen. Zooming in makes it
bigger; zooming out makes it smaller. Graphics
programs have a magnifying-glass tool with which you
can zoom a portion of the screen. The zoom box, the
Mac's equivalent of the **Maximize button** in Windows,
causes a window to return to full size.